A Couple's Guide to Sexual Addiction

A STEP-BY-STEP PLAN TO REBUILD TRUST & RESTORE INTIMACY

PALDROM CATHARINE COLLINS AND GEORGE N. COLLINS, MA

Member of the Society for the Advancement of Sexual Health

Adam[illegible]dia

New York London Toronto Sydney New Delhi

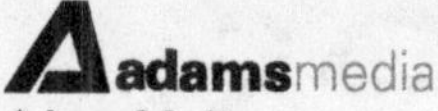

Adams Media
An Imprint of Simon & Schuster, Inc.
57 Littlefield Street
Avon, Massachusetts 02322

For information about special discounts for bulk purchases, please contact Simon & Schuster Special Sales at 1-866-506-1949 or business@simonandschuster.com.

The Simon & Schuster Speakers Bureau can bring authors to your live event. For more information or to book an event contact the Simon & Schuster Speakers Bureau at 1-866-248-3049 or visit our website at www.simonspeakers.com.

Manufactured in the United States of America

10 9 8

Library of Congress Cataloging-in-Publication Data has been applied for.

ISBN 978-1-4405-1221-6
ISBN 978-1-4405-2697-8 (ebook)

This book is intended as general information only, and should not be used to diagnose or treat any health condition. In light of the complex, individual, and specific nature of health problems, this book is not intended to replace professional medical advice. The ideas, procedures, and suggestions in this book are intended to supplement, not replace, the advice of a trained medical professional. Consult your physician before adopting any of the suggestions in this book, as well as about any condition that may require diagnosis or medical attention. The authors and publisher disclaim any liability arising directly or indirectly from the use of this book.

This publication is designed to provide accurate and authoritative information with regard to the subject matter covered. It is sold with the understanding that the publisher is not engaged in rendering legal, accounting, or other professional advice. If legal advice or other expert assistance is required, the services of a competent professional person should be sought.

—From a Declaration of Principles jointly adopted by a Committee of the American Bar Association and a Committee of Publishers and Associations

Many of the designations used by manufacturers and sellers to distinguish their products are claimed as trademarks. Where those designations appear in this book and Simon & Schuster, Inc., was aware of a trademark claim, the designations have been printed with initial capital letters.

We dedicate this book to our dear friend Andrew Adleman, with unending gratitude for his support, guidance, encouragement, and love.

ACKNOWLEDGMENTS

First, we would like to thank and acknowledge Katie Corcoran Lytle at Adams Media. This book was her brainchild and would not exist without her. Additionally, we are grateful to have been able to work with editor Jennifer Lawler, who is an accomplished writer of self-help books.

Special thanks go to all of our colleagues at Compulsion Solutions, James Gallegos, Greg Brian, and particularly Faye Reitman. Faye has been a special support in the writing of this book. For that and for everything Faye brings to our world, we are especially grateful.

We would not have been able to write this book without the support, help, and encouragement of Andrew Adleman. We often speculate that he may be a saint disguised as a skillful author and editor.

Without our teachers, counselors, and guides we would not have had the knowledge, courage, or wisdom to write this book. The words thank you seem too simple to express the fullness of our ever-deepening gratitude.

Finally, we thank our friends and clients who continue to teach and inspire us.

CONTENTS

INTRODUCTION

If you have this book in your hands, you are probably moving through a very difficult passage in your relationship. Perhaps you are certain, or maybe you suspect, that your partner has been sexually unfaithful and you are concerned that an addiction to sex has caused it. Or you may suspect that you have a problem with sexual compulsivity that is causing you to act out sexually in addictive ways that are damaging to your relationship. Your compulsive thoughts or behaviors are creating a barrier to the intimate connection you'd like to have with your partner.

Sexual addiction does not always result in infidelity to the relationship, nor is all sexual infidelity driven by sex addiction. However, sex addiction or compulsivity blocks loving intimacy inside a committed partnership.

Generally, it is the male of the couple who has an issue with sexual addiction. However, please keep in mind that women can also have these issues. Or you may be a same-sex couple. As you read, if the pronouns we are using in any of the descriptions don't fit your situation, please adjust them. This book is for you, too.

It is probably clear to you that you are not connecting with your partner as you would like. But how can you tell if your partner is being gripped by sex addiction in some form? You may have a sense that something is wrong, but you don't know what it might be. Some signs that sex or porn addiction may be playing a part are:

- Your partner is spending a lot of "private" time on the computer.
- He is less available, less communicative with you than he has been in the past.
- He is unusually secretive.

- He does not initiate sex.
- He frequently can't climax sexually.
- He wants to have sex all the time; he's never satisfied.
- You feel a lack of partnership or true intimacy.

If you or your partner is addicted to sex, then sexually compulsive behavior has caused a breach in your relationship. But you can do something about it that can create positive changes. This book is here to help you traverse the shock, the pain, the anger, the fear, and the sadness of what you have discovered and to help you as a couple navigate these troubled waters. You may feel like you are at a crossroads, and that a wrong turn will lead to more pain and suffering.

Trust your instincts. You may not know exactly where your relationship is headed right now. You may have a list of reasons why you should stay, but somehow feel you should leave. This book is written for those couples who are choosing to stay together (at least for now) to work through the difficulties of sexual addiction.

You may be able to use this stormy crisis to make your relationship closer, deeper, and more intimate. But even if you eventually choose to leave, both partners can still benefit from understanding the dynamics that have gotten you to this point in your lives.

At this juncture, even though you may be choosing to stay in the relationship, you probably have many thoughts, feelings, and questions swirling through your head.

Questions for you may include:

- How can I be with this man after what he's done?
- How do I know he won't do it again?
- How do I not monitor his every move?

- How can I ever trust him again?
- Why didn't I recognize and acknowledge what was going on before now?

Questions for him may include:
- Can she ever forgive me?
- Can I forgive myself?
- How can I possibly be with this woman?
- How can I be with her after the rush of what I have been doing?

Reading the information presented here and working through the exercises will help you find your way to the answers not only to these questions but also to the questions that will arise as you learn more about sexual compulsion/addiction and how that plays inside your relationship dynamic.

Work through the exercises in the book gradually. Rushing doesn't help. It takes time to unravel and rebuild your relationship. Be compassionate and patient with yourself and your partner. And yes, this book will show you how to do that, too!

The examples, anecdotes, stories, letters, and e-mails you will find in this book are fictionalized composites of the individuals and couples we have known and worked with. We have made every effort to maintain anonymity. If a story seems to be the account of someone you know, it could be due to the fact that the details of sexual compulsion are so common and pervasive, with very familiar patterns.

In Part 1 of the book, "Coming to Terms with Your New Reality," we will look at some basic facts about sex addiction and how to live through the initial discovery of the problem of sexual compulsivity in your relationship. In Part 2, "Rebuilding Your

Relationship," we will explore the skills and tools you will need to put the pieces of your partnership back together and to deepen your relationship. Finally, in Part 3, "Moving Forward," we will look at ways to deepen intimacy both emotionally and sexually and how to find outside support if you need it.

PART ONE

COMING TO TERMS WITH YOUR NEW REALITY

CHAPTER 1

Sex Addiction: Really?

Jeannine and Jay, both divorced, met when they were in their late thirties. For almost three years, they had what they felt was a magical relationship. Jeannine had never had such a fulfilling sexual connection as the one she had with Jay.

It was after she'd invited Jay's mother for an extended stay that their sex life seemed to grind to a halt. Jay started staying later and later at work—or so he claimed. The truth was that he was going out for a couple of drinks with his coworkers, then returning to the office to look at porn and masturbate. Though Jay felt ashamed and embarrassed about what he was doing, he didn't understand what was happening or how to stop. He longed to find a way to reconnect with Jeannine, but didn't know how. They began to fight more and more often, over what seemed to be minor matters.

Finally, Jeannine confronted Jay. She told him she didn't know exactly what he was doing at work every night, but she was pretty sure he was having an affair. She told him she was unwilling to live this way and asked him to move out—she was finished. After first denying that anything was going on, Jay finally told her about the porn. He confessed that although he kept promising himself he wouldn't go back to view more porn, each night he did. He admitted that he didn't understand how he had gotten so caught up in the porn.

Discovering Sexual Compulsivity in Your Relationship

Every day we get phone calls and e-mails from individuals and couples who are experiencing infidelity in their relationships, whether through affairs, excessive viewing of porn (while masturbating), engaging prostitutes, visiting massage parlors that specialize in sexual massage, indulging in sexually intriguing chats online or in e-mails, or through some other form of compulsive sexual expression. When they discover what is happening, they feel betrayed. Many say they feel as if they have run with full force into a brick wall. A period of shock—for both partners—often follows. Being discovered as a sexual addict can be as difficult as discovering your partner is a sexual addict. Certainly not every betrayal is due to sexual compulsivity or addiction, but a pattern of betrayal may include sex addiction as a factor.

While some people become aware of the problem in one horrible instant of discovery, often the understanding can creep up in a series of small awakenings. The betrayed partner may have voiced suspicions that were repeatedly denied but which, over time, added up to a certainty.

No matter how you learn about your partner's sexual addiction, it is a stunning and painful revelation. You may feel shocked or numb, hurt, ashamed, afraid, and angry. Your partner may also feel shocked or numb, hurt, ashamed, afraid, and sometimes angry. In fact, the real brick wall you have run into may well be a wall of shame about the behavior of your partner, your behavior, your inability to stop the behavior, or a lack of awareness that it was happening. Shame is a significant aspect of sexual addiction that will be explored in greater detail in Chapter 6.

What Sexual Addiction Is

Sex addiction is a compulsive urge to engage in sexual activity, thoughts, or fantasies in a way that is detrimental to the individual, his family, his friends, and/or his work. It blocks the development of true intimacy in a relationship. Sex addiction is also labeled sexual dependency or sexual compulsivity. For the ease of communication here, we will interchangeably use the terms sex addiction, sexual compulsivity, or sexual dependency to refer to this issue.

Our natural urge for sex, the way sex is used for marketing purposes, and the explosion of porn on the Internet have created a "perfect storm" of conditions leading to sex addiction.

To understand how sexual addiction can arise, it helps to understand what impulses and motivations drive the behavior.

The Sexual Impulse

As a human, you have an animal body guided by instinct. You also have a reasoning part of your brain that allows you to work with your instinctive responses. In its basic and natural form—if there has not been physical or emotional damage along the way—human sexual contact feels good, touching feels good, having an orgasm feels good. This is normal and wonderful. The natural desire for sex and sexual pleasure is not an enemy. The natural sexual impulse can guide you to finding closeness, connectedness, and intimacy with your partner.

When your natural biochemical responses produce hormonal impulses, you experience sexual desire. When sexual urges get misdirected or they become addictive or compulsive, instead of leading to pleasure and connection, the sex drive can lead to suffering.

Basically, we all want to love and be loved. At the core of our humanity, we yearn to be treated with kindness and compassion and to return kindness and compassion. And we quite naturally require human connection at a biological level. We have evolved as members of a tribe, as part of a society. We need each other.

Biology and Sex

Our needs for sex, touch, attachment, bonding, and commitment are chemically influenced in different ways at different stages of our lives. The hormone testosterone, sometimes called "the warrior hormone," is found in both men and women. Men, however, tend to have twenty to forty times more testosterone than women. Testosterone creates an urge for sexual contact, but may also foster the desire to dominate and to be alone. Thus, it's no surprise that men are more inclined to one-night stands—or that they like to roll over and go to sleep afterward.

In men, testosterone levels peak in the morning and are lower at night. They cycle up and down every fifteen to twenty minutes. It is widely known that at puberty young men are hit with a flood of testosterone. Testosterone also spikes for young women at puberty, but women produce more of the hormone estrogen. Estrogen causes a woman to want to be held, and causes her to feel receptive to sexual advances.

Touch and the chemicals released with touch also play a vital role in our survival, happiness, and our experience of connectedness. Studies have shown that babies do not thrive and can die when there is a lack of touch. As we grow older, without touch we become more subject to senility and can die sooner. Touching and being touched by someone alters our chemical composition, strengthening the biochemical bond with that individual. Even a thought of the person can cause a hormonal surge. A chemical reaction occurs that actually causes a craving for more touch from that individual. In this way, touching and being touched are literally addictive.

The physical structures in your brain also influence how you respond to the world. The prefrontal cortex, which sits right behind your forehead, is associated with personality, intelligence, ethics, and morality, and with regulating control over emotional and sexual urges.

In other words, you can override the primitive call-of-the-wild automatic responses we all have that compel us to get away from pain and danger and to move toward pleasure. Studies have shown that we can engage the thinking function of the prefrontal cortex by something as simple as using our thinking function to label an angry face as "angry."

By putting just a little bit of awareness around your automatic survival response, you can begin to have a choice about the response. This is one of the vital components of overcoming sexual addiction. By understanding your biological influences, you can start to work with your urges and impulses as they arise. You can begin to see how your biology naturally creates a desire for sexual connectedness or a desire to masturbate or a desire to dominate or a desire to be receptive to sex or a desire to touch and be touched. You can begin to find ways to work with these energies so they do not overwhelm your relationship. You can find ways to work with your biochemistry so your desires for attachment, connection, bonding, and commitment can be met.

Pornography

Because of the way our hormonal impulses can drive our behaviors, sex has also become entangled with power and domination, which is at odds with our need for closeness, touch, and connection. The portrayal of sex as a matter of power and domination is a common theme in much of porn. This can create a distortion and confusion about sexual impulses and what is actually desirable for women. Those who have viewed a lot of pornography can start to imagine that women in real life are like the women portrayed in pornography. This is one way that sexual compulsion can damage relationships.

Viewing porn can be instantly gratifying. It's readily available and doesn't require connection or cooperation. Testosterone drives the urge for sexual expression, and men seem to be more oriented to being aroused and attracted visually. In particular, when sexually explicit materials are introduced (or discovered) during puberty, a cycle of connecting with the sexual excitement and release that comes with the viewing of pornography can be set in motion in a way that impacts the view of and approach to sexuality for many years to come. The natural maturing of the capacities for sexual connection through truly intimate contact can become diverted.

In 1953, the face of pornography changed with the first issue of *Playboy* magazine. *Playboy* and its related magazines brought pornography into more public—and widespread—view at magazine stands everywhere. These objectified and sexualized images of women were packaged as a lifestyle choice available to any successful and intellectual gentleman. *Playboy* and *Penthouse* magazine vied to produce the most sexually explicit material. In 1974, with the publishing of *Hustler* magazine, the limits of what was acceptable for mainstream distribution were pushed even further, laying the groundwork for the multibillion dollar porn industry of today.

With the explosion of Internet porn—and computers to view it on—porn is now accessible in ways it never was before. Any kind of pornographic material that can be imagined (or desired) is available instantly in the privacy of one's home or office. Greater accessibility has also led to more explicit and increasingly violent material aimed at younger audiences. Currently, the average age at which a child first views porn online is eleven—and what a child sees is a far cry from that first edition of *Playboy*.

It is no secret that pornography tends to depict sexuality from a view that objectifies. Many of our clients have found it difficult to understand that the view of sex portrayed by porn is a fantasy. It is a type of fairy tale created for men by the porn industry because sex sells. That doesn't mean porn is necessarily bad. Sometimes couples can use it as part of a healthy sex life. For example, sexually explicit materials that depict partners sexually connecting and caring for each other can model the connection that is possible through human sexuality. However, an individual who compulsively uses pornography generally needs to abstain from viewing pornography completely.

The Label "Sex Addict"

Many people resist the "sex addict" label. They don't want to associate addiction with their behaviors or with their relationship. Sometimes it's easier for people to think they simply have a bad habit. We encourage them, and encourage you, not to get stuck on words, but to focus on healing. Whether we use the label bad habit, addiction, compulsion, or dependency, or any other words, if your behavior is creating suffering, then you have a problem. For the individual who is caught by sexual compulsion, sex has become something other than an intimate expression of loving connectedness. The pleasure that is inherently present in orgasm or connection with another has been altered and is being used as a balm, an escape, a distraction, rather than being enjoyed for what it does offer.

Unfortunately, shying away from the phrase "sex addiction" can keep you from the very information that can be helpful. If you know what sex addiction means, then if you are suffering from it (or your partner is), you can recognize that you're not alone and you can find help and relief for the pain that compulsive behavior causes.

Just because someone likes to masturbate or to have sex doesn't mean that he or she is a sex addict or has a problem. A friend of ours asked if we thought he had a problem because he loves to look at his fiancée when she is naked, and he really enjoys having sex with her—frequently. We assured him that he is a healthy male.

What Are the Signs of Sexual Addiction?

To determine if you (or your partner) may have a problem with sexual addiction, ask these questions:

1. Are you (or is your partner) preoccupied with sexual thoughts, impulses, or desires?
2. Are your (or is your partner's) sexual behavior(s) getting in the way of having the intimate connection you want to have?
3. Are your (or is your partner's) sexual behavior(s) getting in the way of work or causing financial problems?

If you answered yes to even one of these questions, it is likely that sexual compulsivity is an issue for you. At the very least, you can assume that sexual compulsion is creating problems for you in your life and with your relationship.

You have an issue with sex addiction, dependency, or compulsion if your sexual behaviors interfere with your day-to-day living by causing stress on your family members, friends, other loved ones, and/or work. If your sexual expression has become self-defeating, then you have a problem. If your sexual behaviors are getting in the way of intimacy, then you have a problem.

Your natural animal instinct to soothe yourself with this particular type of behavior is overriding your capacity to regulate your impulses in a way that allows for human connection and intimacy.

The problem with soothing yourself with sexual behavior is that the soothing is momentary. You may feel ashamed, too, because you are probably aware that your behavior is out of your control. An internal war is going on. Life is not working. As George likes to describe the cycle of sexual compulsivity, "You can't get enough of what won't satisfy you."

Porn and Masturbation—"All Men Do It"

If someone says you have sexually addictive behavior, your automatic response may be, "All men do it," "Are you kidding me? This is just how guys are wired," or "This doesn't have anything to do with my relationship. It's no big deal."

But if you could let go of the defensiveness for a moment, you would probably say something like, "Please don't make me stop. I really need this. This is the one thing I can count on to never let me down."

It's easy to understand that when one of the partners in a committed relationship has an affair the behavior is harmful to the relationship and is unacceptable. But when you're simply masturbating, you may wonder, "What's the harm in that? If the sexual impulse is so natural, then why would following it create a problem?"

Let's dig into this. Start with a natural, run-of-the-mill instinctive sexual urge—just an urge on its own, not connected to feeling close and loving toward someone—just that nice warm sexual urge that kind of glows in your genital area. At its most simple, that urge is the desire to feel the release and pleasure in an orgasm. So the individual masturbates and has an orgasm. It just feels good, and there isn't a problem.

Most of us masturbate; that's not the problem. The problem occurs when masturbation interferes with our relationships. Most of us have sexual thoughts and feelings about people we see and meet that we find sexually attractive. Again, that's not a problem. It only becomes a problem when you're driven to engage in sexual behaviors that interfere with the rest of your life.

Someone who does not have an issue with sexual compulsivity might have a hard time understanding it. A man who isn't addicted to pornography can look at porn, even be stimulated by it, but he will not need to go back to it day after day. As one such man reported to us, "When I look at porn, after about fifteen minutes it just gets kind of boring. I'd much rather have sex with my wife."

Sexually Compulsive or "Normal"?

If you're sexually addicted, your behavior may include the compulsion to view Internet porn and masturbate, but generally, it doesn't end there. For example, the sexually compulsive man goes to lunch and sees a pretty waitress wearing a tight T-shirt and a short skirt. Now, almost any man is going to notice how attractive she is and might even be sexually aroused, but the sexually compulsive man will take it further. He will try to give her his business card. He will imagine having sex with her. Then he will take the memory of her out of the restaurant with him. He'll remember what she said, how she said it, and he will imagine that she wants to have sex with him. Then he might take it even further. When he gets back to his office or when he gets home that night, he will search the Internet for a porn video of someone who resembles her so he can masturbate to her memory. Even if he doesn't like the restaurant, he may go back over and over again, just to talk with her to continue his fantasy. She may even tell him that she is not interested in a relationship with him, but his fantasy will continue.

A sex addict can find it difficult to reconcile that when he masturbates to porn he is not having sex with a real person, or when he goes to a prostitute he is not in an actual relationship. Many times clients have been surprised and hurt to learn that the interest their prostitute "girlfriend" is feigning is based on the money she is being paid. The "guy gets girl" happy ending with the prostitute only happens in the movies—it's just another one of those fairy tales.

An average guy can look up the sports scores on his computer without being compelled to go to his browser's hidden bookmarks that lead to porn. He doesn't need to step into the bathroom for a quick release before an important meeting. He doesn't need to position his computer away from the door to ensure that someone coming in won't catch him looking at something sexually explicit. He doesn't need to wipe the history and cookies from his Internet browser several times a day to avoid detection.

The average guy is not troubled by his interest in sex. He enjoys having sex. He doesn't need to keep his sexual thoughts, actions, and fantasies a secret from his partner. The sexually compulsive individual knows that his secret sex life is keeping him from the connection that is possible. He just doesn't know how to limit (and stop) the sexual behaviors that are getting in the way of intimacy with his partner.

Admitting a Problem Exists

The key, as with so many other areas in our lives, is to first recognize and admit that a problem exists. Recognizing this can help you uncover the roots of your self-destructive behaviors.

For example, when Dan, a successful manager of public works projects in his early thirties, first came to see us, his relationship with his girlfriend had blown up after she discovered that he had been texting, instant messaging, and then meeting couples to have sex with them. His story began with the use of Internet porn, which escalated into more risky behaviors.

After several months of counseling, he began to see the underlying feelings of worthlessness that were driving his actions, a kind of panic response. He understood how he had been attempting to lessen his uncomfortable feeling with the distraction and rush of masturbating to Internet porn and having sex with couples.

At that moment, he said, "I'm not a sex addict, I'm just trying to get away from this painful feeling." While he did not want to admit to the label, he had clearly seen that his addictive behaviors were a cover-up for the actual problem.

Is Dan a sex addict? Yes, he certainly has an issue with sexual compulsivity. He will always need to remember how he has picked a whole range of sexual distractions as his coping strategies. Until he is further along in his recovery, these coping strategies (e.g., sexual acting out) will probably continue to arise automatically when he feels hurt, angry, lonely, or tired.

Why Me?

In counseling, we mostly see men who are acting out sexually with porn, prostitutes, and/or serial affairs. These can certainly be issues for women as well, but we're describing the general trend. We're often asked why some people seem to have a weakness in connecting intimately and sexually. Why do certain people get caught up in acting out sexually while others do not? It appears to be a combination of life experience interacting with the natural animal survival impulses—a combination of nature and nurture.

Sexualization and Objectification

It's neither a secret nor a revelation that our society sexualizes and objectifies women. Sexuality is used to get our attention, to promote, and to sell. In advertising for milk, cars, and sports, we are bombarded by images of women's breasts, legs, and hair. Men and women alike are inundated with such sexualized images and messages.

In our practice, we have found that many of the men who have issues with sexual compulsion have been taught in a quite overt way to view women through a sexual lens. These men have heard highly sexual messages about women from their fathers or from their older brothers or friends, such as how good it is to "get a lot of pussy." For example, our client Jeff described how his dad told him to go ahead and have sex with women whenever he could. "However," he warned Jeff, "be sure and use a condom."

A young man learns from his father, his friends, and from the society around him. Jeff's father had a stash of *Playboy* magazines that he hid under the bed. Jeff's father alerted Jeff to take note how he would put a twenty-dollar bill on the mantle for Jeff's mother whenever "she gave him some."

If a young man's father looks at young girls in a sexual way, the son notices. When Jeff was thirteen, his father shared with him that he was in love with the daughter of a family friend, Jeff's thirteen-year-old classmate and friend. The father confided in Jeff, "I think it could work out with her." So as Jeff was first feeling the blush of his budding sexuality, he learned that women were there to have sex with whenever you can, that even his thirteen-year-old female friends should be considered in this light.

It is not so surprising that when Jeff came to us, even though he loved his wife dearly, he was fixated on masturbating to porn on the Internet. He and his wife were dismayed by the fact that he couldn't really be sexually passionate with her. He only felt safe and connected to the images on the computer. And his image of choice for viewing pornography was girls who looked to be about thirteen.

Even in less overtly damaging situations, boys and girls alike are surrounded by sexualized messages. This kind of thinking keeps us in the realm of fantasy, which tends to focus on appearances. The "men will be men" overlay, the image of the hookers and strippers at the bachelor party, is a widely known and widely accepted stereotype. There are regular reports of prostitutes being available as a reward for men in high-rolling business circles. This seems to be an accepted part of the world in which we live.

It is often noted that men sexualize and objectify women, but it may not be as readily apparent how women sexualize and objectify themselves and other women. You probably have noted how men tend to be stimulated visually. Women are aware of that fact. Because of the ways women are biochemically wired, they are influenced both consciously and unconsciously by how they feel they are being viewed. Although each of us as humans are aware of our appearance and how that appearance influences others' perception of our value, women are particularly subject to this pressure. We have found that for women, the focus on physical appearance can often manifest in issues around food and eating or around shopping and spending.

It can be helpful for both partners to recognize the influence of sexualization and objectification. We have found that in most relationships, there are times when each of the partners feels that they are not being seen for who they really are. In fact, it would be a miracle if this didn't happen. Each one of us is impacted by physical and biochemical influences. We each have been subject to the influences of our family upbringing, even in the most idyllic of circumstances. We are each a product of the cultural influences around us. We are subject to all of the objectification that comes with being human.

CHAPTER SUMMARY

- Sex addiction is a compulsive urge to engage in sexual activities, thoughts, or fantasies in a way that is detrimental to the individual, his family, his friends, and/or his work. It blocks the development of true intimacy in a relationship.
- For someone caught by sexual compulsion, sex has become something other than an intimate expression of loving connectedness. The pleasure that is inherently present in orgasm or connection with another has been altered and is being used as a balm, an escape, a distraction, rather than being enjoyed for what it does offer.
- The sexually compulsive individual may know that his secret sex life is keeping him from the connection he wants to have. He just doesn't know how to limit (and stop) the sexual behaviors that are getting in the way of intimacy with his partner.

- The natural urge for sex, the way sex is used for marketing purposes, and the explosion of porn on the Internet have created a "perfect storm" of conditions that lead to sex addiction.
- To understand how sex addiction can become a problem, it helps to understand the impulses and motivations that drive the behavior. Gaining understanding about these influences, it is possible to work with the urges and impulses as they arise.

Looking Forward

In Chapter 2, we'll talk about what happens when you first discover sexual addiction in your relationship (either your own addiction or your partner's), and we'll show you how to begin the healing.

CHAPTER 2

Getting Past the Shock

It is difficult to get along with another person. As the joy and ease that comes with falling in love fades, our natural defenses, opinions, and protective mechanisms appear more frequently. When the glow of the new relationship is gone, the real relationship emerges. We enter the territory of our unhealed wounding. We expect that our relationship will be the place where our wounds will be healed—and that is a possibility—but the healing generally occurs in ways we might not expect.

While sexual relationships can be a way to connect during the times of tension that can arise between partners, it is also a place of great vulnerability. We bare ourselves to each other in our sexual connecting. While the feelings that arise around connecting sexually can be quite tender, when we add addictive behavior into the already vulnerable area of our sexual connection, we have the ingredients for conflict and suffering.

It can be difficult for some partners to clearly articulate their needs and views, especially about sexual needs, feelings, and desires. Sexuality is openly touted in the media, yet the layer of taboo that can also be a part of our internalized structures frequently hampers open, meaningful conversation. When the elements of vulnerability and feelings about privacy are combined with the powerful force of sexuality, and then sexually compulsive behavior is thrown into the mix, it's no wonder that a potentially explosive situation occurs.

The Shock of Discovery

However you have arrived at the circumstances that have drawn you to read these words, know that you are not alone. Whatever feelings and emotions arise for you, be they shock, numbness, hurt, shame, fear, anger—whatever you may be feeling—your feelings are normal. You may feel all of these feelings or none of them. Of course, you may have feelings that you shouldn't act on, but the feelings themselves are simply a natural response to a painful situation. What is especially important in this moment is knowing that you will be able to tolerate the feelings you are having, as strong and painful as they may be.

In Chapter 7, we will more fully describe the process of working with strong feelings and emotions in a way that can potentially deepen your connection with yourself and with your partner. For now, just know that you are going to survive the shock of this time.

Initially, it is not necessary to attempt to try to understand the inner workings of what has happened; it is enough to simply experience your reactions. It may feel counterintuitive to you in this moment, but the most powerful stance you can take right now is to become even more vulnerable. By this, we mean that if you are the partner who has been hurt, now is the time to speak directly about how you are hurt. Speaking about your pain and disappointment will be much more powerfully received if you do not attack. Don't label or diagnose your partner, and don't generalize about his character flaws. As much as possible, accurately describe and convey whatever emotion you are having.

If you are the partner who has acted out, this is the time to be vulnerable enough to really listen to your partner's hurt. Emotions and feelings are usually quite strong during this time—anger, fear, sadness, and grief may feel like they will never be finished, but we promise, they will. The most skillful stance you can take is to allow yourself to be a bendable tree in very strong wind. In those moments when you feel you will be overcome, close your eyes, breathe deeply, and picture yourself bending but not breaking.

Sexual Compulsivity and Intimate Sex Are Not the Same

Compulsive or addictive sex is not the same thing as natural loving sex. Compulsive sexual behavior occurs when the natural drive to connect sexually (and the pleasure associated with that connection and activity) becomes subverted and is used as an avoidance or simply a release rather than as an expression of intimate connection. Sexually compulsive behavior can occur in sexual contact with a committed partner, but most often it is indulged in and acted out either with images (generally pornography) or with live people. Compulsive sex is not training wheels for intimate sex. A man who regularly and compulsively looks at porn and masturbates is not increasing his capacity to connect intimately and sexually with his partner.

The experience of intimate sex is based on a connection born of vulnerability, trust (built through honesty), and compassionate connection. We regularly counsel that the primary ingredients required for moving from sexual compulsion are the desire to stop the sexually compulsive behaviors and the willingness to build trust and vulnerability with your partner through undefended honesty. We will address the building of these skills in the chapters that follow.

The first thing you need to do is stabilize your relationship, which has been damaged by sexual compulsivity. This stabilization will help your connection remain afloat while you navigate these troubled waters. This is your immediate first aid. We encourage both of you to read what we have to say to each of you. No matter which side of what can appear to be a very wide and deep chasm you find yourself standing, no matter which of you has been caught by sexual compulsivity, this information can be helpful to you right now.

For Her Right Now: Accepting Your Emotions

While deeper understanding takes time, it's important to understand right now that whatever has happened, whatever your partner is doing or has done, you did not cause it. It is not your fault. You certainly may have done something (inadvertently or even deliberately) that has caused your partner to feel unhappy, uncomfortable, angry, or afraid. You quite probably have bumped into some tender emotional places in him and that particular contact has caused him to feel the full brunt of a reaction he does not want to feel. This does not mean that you are responsible for the way he has chosen to deal with his discomfort. You actually do not have the power to make that kind of a choice for your partner. In a way, that may be a relief!

Your partner's sexual compulsivity is not about you, but you are deeply affected by it; it impacts you directly. However, you cannot mend the pieces inside your partner that are preventing his lack of ability to connect to you intimately. The repair he needs to do will be an "inside job," meaning it must happen within. Even if you may want to, you cannot do it for him. You may support and witness his healing, but he will do the mending of his capacity to connect intimately with you.

Although you cannot directly change him, this does not mean you aren't involved. You are involved. This is personal. It is not possible for you to feel otherwise. What you can do is communicate your hurt clearly and without attack.

One of our clients, after her husband lost his job because he was arrested for soliciting prostitutes in the company vehicle, threw her wedding ring off the Golden Gate Bridge. Perhaps you have reacted in a similarly expressive manner. Many women simply don't know how to respond. They report feeling frozen or numb. They don't want their relationship to end, but they know the relationship they now have is not workable.

Whatever your initial response, it does not predict the future of your relationship. It may seem surprising, but the woman who threw her ring off the bridge ultimately forged a new and more intimate relationship with her husband.

You are absolutely correct in your feeling that he is taking his sexual energy outside of your relationship. This is a betrayal even if it does not involve others. Although it is generally easier to work through the betrayal that occurs with compulsive use of pornography, the intimacy that you would like to have with your partner is not available to you when he is indulging in *any* manner of sexual compulsivity.

To the extent that you can be compassionate with yourself for whatever you may be feeling, you will also be able to be compassionate with your partner. Lovingly and gently allowing yourself to feel your hurt benefits both of you and your relationship. This does not mean you have permission to demean him in the name of "sharing your feelings." However, you should allow yourself to deeply experience whatever it is you are feeling. Even though there may be a multitude of strong feelings and emotions, and even though it may seem that you cannot withstand your feelings, we want to assure you that you can. Chapter 7 directly addresses how to work with your strong feelings and emotions.

You do not need to rush to get over your experience of betrayal. There is no timeline for resolving your feelings. We have seen that attempting to keep yourself from feeling your painful reactions can actually prolong them.

What counts now, more than ever, is trusting what you think and feel. This may be a crash course in learning to trust yourself. You don't need to do what you don't want to do. You don't need to become a porn substitute. You do not need to be sexual if you do not want to. You can ask clearly for what you need during this time without criticizing or condemning your partner. It can be helpful to keep in mind that he is hurting, too. What he has done is unacceptable, but this does not mean that he is unacceptable.

For now, you may find it comforting to be able to monitor his e-mail accounts, computer access, cell phone calls, or other portals that he has used to indulge his sexual compulsivity. If this would create a greater sense of safety for you, then ask for it. However, in the long run, you do not want to set yourself up to be viewed by your partner as his supervisor, or as the sexual or porn police. Since you cannot cure or fix your partner, we generally advise that you not become an overseer of his activities. Besides, we have found that monitoring in this way doesn't work. Most of the sexually compulsive men we have worked with can figure out how to get around any filter, barrier, or other monitoring system if they want to. Just know that, ultimately, what you really want and need is intimacy; and that intimacy will be built through honesty and vulnerability—of both partners. Chapter 8 deals more specifically with the importance of rebuilding trust through undefended honesty.

Finally, hold whatever compassion you can muster for yourself and for this issue in your relationship—the problem will not end overnight. Whatever your reaction is, whatever feelings come up for you, however you may respond, you have the capacity to work with your feelings and emotions. You may respond by feeling the need to be alone, to be in nature, or to express. However you have responded so far, even if it has not been pretty, forgive yourself.

We have seen over and over again how moving through the blockages to intimacy that are revealed by healing your relationship (although at times extremely rocky and challenging) can bring your relationship back from what may appear to be certain disaster. Healing can take place in all kinds of circumstances—as evidenced by the following story of Julia and Kyle. While this story tells of a wife's reaction that we put into the category of "do not attempt this at home," we share it with you so you can see how even a relationship that appears to be beyond repair can come back from the brink.

Julia and Kyle

Having been married twice before, Julia was determined that her marriage to Kyle would fare better than her previous attempts. Julia knew that Kyle liked porn and that he had brought a very large box of porn videos with him when they moved into their new home. However, she had thought they could look at the videos together and it might be fun. After several months, Julia realized that Kyle was not very interested in watching the videos with her or even in having sex with her.

Kyle would tell Julia he was tired, yet she saw that he had energy to work, golf, go bowling, and play baseball. She began finding pornographic materials where he had tried to hide them in the bedroom. He complained that she didn't go out very much and he wanted more privacy. Julia realized that he wanted more privacy so he could masturbate to porn.

Julia even heard from a mutual friend who said that Kyle had called him one night and said, "I don't know what to do. Julia wants me to have sex with her and won't leave me alone." The mutual friend had responded, "Your problem is that your wife wants to have sex with you?"

The friend did not understand the grip of sexual compulsion, and how it was not allowing Kyle to glimpse the possibility of intimate, connected sex with his very real wife. Those porn videos were Kyle's "girlfriends." He knew they would never criticize him or let him down.

As Kyle grew more distant from Julia, she knew their relationship was slipping away, but she felt powerless. Julia's frustration—including sexual frustration—with Kyle continued. She felt like she was competing with the porn videos. Whenever she complained to Kyle about the videos, she felt that he just tuned her out. She felt as if nothing she could do or say was getting through to Kyle.

One night after Kyle had gone to bed after making more excuses for refusing sex with her, Julia finally had had enough. She gathered up all of Kyle's pornographic videos, which filled a huge box. She dragged the box into the garage and dumped it on the concrete floor. She found a hatchet they used when camping and hit the videos until they began to break apart. Her frustration poured out as she kept smashing the videos into smaller pieces.

Although she had no prior plan, Julia next gathered up the pieces and put them into all the things she felt Kyle loved more than her. She poured pieces into his bowling bag, his golf bag, his baseball-equipment bag, and then finally she filled his car with chopped-up porn videos.

Julia's actions got Kyle's attention, even though her way of doing so was rather drastic. They began counseling, and each of them was slowly able to gain more perspective on how to build true intimacy. They were able to begin to communicate more openly and honestly. Kyle was able to share that he had interpreted Julia's request for sexual intimacy as Julia saying he was not doing a good job or he was "not enough." He was able to see that his connection to the porn was actually preventing his developing sexual intimacy with his wife. He was able to see how it was easier and more comfortable for him to masturbate to porn rather than deal with Julia's real relationship requests or what he considered her criticisms.

Julia realized that she needed to look at her fears of relationships failing, which were a reflection of self-esteem issues. Together, they were able to see how each of their behaviors influenced the other person and contributed to the issues between them. Kyle had to first be willing to look at his compulsive use of porn and to seek support in learning how to move from compulsive sex to intimate, connected sex. The bond of their relationship was strong enough for each of them to be willing to look at how they were negatively impacting each other. The willingness they each had was the basis for the courage needed to build true vulnerability, trust, and intimacy. As they say, it takes two to tango. And they were finally learning to dance—with each other.

For Him Right Now: Acknowledging What Has Happened

Imagine for a moment what it would be like if the roles in your relationship were reversed. What if your wife was constantly searching for porn sites where the men had sexy, muscled bodies? What if she was masturbating to those images? How would you feel if you found out your wife was paying younger men to have sex with her, either virtually on the Internet or in person? Would you doubt your masculinity? Even a little bit? Or maybe a lot? Would it change how you felt about the possibility of having sex with your wife?

What if she had told you many times that she was going to stop, but only now was she declaring that her marriage to you was what mattered and she would really stop this time? What if, after all her confessions, you found out some truths that she had not told you? Perhaps she had not revealed the hundreds or even thousands of dollars of the family's money she had spent on attempting to fulfill her sexually compulsive behavior.

Even if you have stopped acting out sexually, what you did before is not going to be forgiven overnight, and it may never be forgotten. But it happened, so the best thing for you to do is stop denying the extent of the problem, both to yourself and to her. How would you feel if you learned she had been lying to you, possibly for years? If she was the sex addict who was lost in sexually compulsive behavior and, as a result, was out of touch in your relationship, how easily could you confide in her, trust her, and share your real feelings with her?

Committing to Reality—Not Fantasy

What you need to know right now is that it is possible to move beyond what has happened and work toward solidifying your relationship with the woman in your life. But you need to be honest with yourself. The real question is, do you want to stop living in fantasies with fantasy women or do you want to experience intimacy with a real woman?

We know how difficult it is to stop. Do you know the one big difference between men who continue to act out sexually and men who have positive intimate relationships with the women in their lives? The men who act out live in fantasy and the men who experience intimate relationships live in reality. The adult entertainment industry, the prostitutes and strip club dancers, all feed on your fantasies. That's why you can never get enough. That's why you're never really satisfied. It's not real.

Are you ready to stop believing the Santa Claus of porn is going to "bring" you the perfect woman? Are you ready to take the necessary steps to salvage your relationship and be a mature adult?

If you have kids, think about them. You may believe your sexually compulsive behavior is private and has no impact on them, but that's another fantasy. Your relationship with your wife has a major influence on how well your children will be able to maintain intimate relationships later in their lives. If they do not see a model for real intimacy and how to relate in an authentic way to another adult, they will not know that skill. It does not happen by magic; it is learned. And they learn it from you—just think about that. If you still insist that your behavior does not impact them, then you are living in denial.

Changing your mind is not easy, but it can be done. Many men have accomplished the same thing. This book is a step toward breaking from your sexually compulsive behavior and learning to connect with another person in a new way. You are more than the compulsive guy who can't stop. You are more than the person who feels bad about himself, who feels shame, pain, and guilt. There is something deeper and more important to you. That part of you can take charge and make change. The part of you that is acting out is just one aspect of you.

Clayton's Experience

Here is what a client named Clayton wrote about his urges to continue to masturbate to porn rather than have sex with his wife: *I have lived with this urge, this compulsion for my entire life, but I also know that it does not need to be this way. Women want to be loved and want to have intimacy just as much as men do. How can I expect to get anything if I do not put anything into my relationship? For my entire marriage I have lived in my own secluded world. I have lived with my stories and in the bathroom. I have lived all of my secrets and all of my lies! They were tales that never ended and were like chameleons that could change shapes and colors just so easily. In the end, what did I get? In the end, I was sitting alone in front of the computer with my pants down and my cock in my hand. Just like I was yesterday, and the day before, and the day before that. I was all alone. I was by myself. My fantasy stories were filling my mind, and that was making my cock hard. When it was over, I was all alone. I was feeling badly. I was feeling guilty. Look, I just do not want this anymore! I do not want those feelings. I do not want any of that. What kind of sex was it that I was having? Was that "hot sex"? Was any of it real? I want more out of my life!*

The point is that you have a major decision to make. Do you want to pretend that you're changing so the woman in your life will stop being angry with you, or do you want to really change so you will go from living in a fantasy world to one where you live in real intimacy with a real person? The following chapters will help you gain the understanding and tools to better understand your sexual behaviors and how to repair your relationship.

For now, we will provide some baseline advice for getting through the next few days and weeks. We understand that you probably do not have enough information or understanding to fully embrace the issues at hand. That's okay for the moment, but we find, especially right now, that it is helpful for you to bolster your listening skills as much as possible.

Listen to Her

You need to listen to your partner so you can actually connect with her and what she is feeling. And you need to not be angry back. You can just listen and not defend yourself. You can feel the words she is saying and the impact your behavior has had on her. This may not be easy, and will most likely be painful, but you can do it. Just remember how you might feel if she was the one having fantasy affairs with incredibly sexy men while leaving you out in the cold.

The point is not to assign blame, but to accept the facts so you can move on toward a closer relationship. In one way, finally being honest is the greatest gift your relationship could ever have. Many relationships are based on lies, and many relationships lack real intimacy. You and the woman in your life have the opportunity for something amazing.

What our clients have ultimately discovered is that real intimacy with a real person is better than you could have imagined, and much better than a fantasy. Again, it is not easy. The women on the porn sites, the prostitutes and strip club dancers—none of them talk back to you. They only take your money and pretend that "you're the man." But you have not been the man. Now is your chance to change all that. Are you ready to make your choice?

What Do You Both Do Right Now?

The bad news is that you both may feel as if your relationship is irrevocably shattered. The good news, as has been learned from many couples that have been through this process, is that most people who threaten to leave don't actually follow through. Even when a couple does separate, the chances are good that they will reunite, provided each is committed to their individual recovery. Disclosure can lay the groundwork for a new relationship, based on honesty and greater intimacy.

Even though you may feel completely miserable, the time is ripe with opportunity. That may sound hard to believe, but the truth is that the information coming to light has presented you with building blocks for a new foundation for your relationship. If the connection between the two of you is strong enough, this can be a time for becoming free of concerns that have been weighing you down your entire life. This is the time to go for it.

Exercise: Making a Commitment to Yourself

One of the difficulties in creating a relationship in today's world is that the roles and rules are not as defined as they have been in the past. As couples, this gives us a lot more freedom to create relationships that really work for us as individuals, even though it can be confusing.

The value of a commitment is that it gets our attention. The commitment we make to another creates a bond that challenges us to become more than the sum of the two parts. At the end of Chapter 8, we will ask you to make a new commitment to each other, but before you can make a new honest and lasting commitment, it is necessary to lay the groundwork by making a true commitment to yourself. This is mandatory so that you can really look into the dynamics within the relationship that are not working. You cannot give something to someone else that you do not have internally. So you begin this process of commitment with yourself.

To do this exercise—and to move forward in your relationship—you need to set some bottom-line rules. The partner who has been sexually compulsive needs to have the desire and willingness to stop the sexually acting-out behavior. This behavior is an ineffective tool he has been using to seek out the closeness we all desire. If the desire and willingness to stop sexually acting out is not in place, then you don't have a basis from which to begin. Additionally, the partner who has been betrayed needs to have the desire and willingness to go through the process of investigation with her partner.

Both partners also need to be willing to begin to look into the dynamics within the relationship system that are not working. What is preventing true intimacy? In what ways are each of the partners contributing to the difficulties in the relationship? How can each partner become more vulnerable in a way that leads to greater intimacy?

Please note that we are not suggesting that a difficulty in the couple's dynamic in any way justifies sexually acting out by either partner.

Find a time to sit down quietly for at least ten minutes in a place where you can write. You can, of course, take longer if you need, but it is important to have time when you know you will not be interrupted. For a few minutes, just breathe in and out and don't try to solve anything or think about anything. Then remember a time or a place when you felt completely safe. Really sink into that feeling of being safe. Now, let yourself know the commitment you want to make to yourself regarding your relationship and record it either on paper or in your computer. It is important that you have a record of your commitment to yourself.

For now, you do not need to figure out specific strategies about how you will carry through with your commitment. In this moment, it is important that you know and see what you value—to what are you willing to commit? Think of this as driving a stake in the ground and claiming the territory of that which you truly value.

Beginning the Healing: Understanding How You Objectify Your Partner

As we discussed in Chapter 1, it's common for people to objectify each other. This plays into the sexual addiction process by making it easier for a person to desire a fantasy rather than deal with messy reality. To deal with messy reality, as you must in order to change your relationship, find ways to go beyond the appearance.

It is possible to shift from relating to and even desiring the outward appearance of a person—the objectification—to appreciating the true beauty of a person. It's a deeper level of beauty and immensely more satisfying than a surface experience. It is a beauty you *can* get enough of—as opposed to objectification, which you can never get enough of and of which the addict is always wanting more. Objectification is not rewarding.

For men who have been engaging in sexually compulsive ways it is important to begin to see how you sexualize and objectify the individuals in images or real life that are the focus of your acting out behavior. Also notice how (and if) you have objectified your partner by seeing her solely through the lens of sexuality or through your view of her based on what you have learned a partner or wife should be.

For women, it is helpful to find the ways that you may objectify as well. Notice how (and if) you have objectified your partner by seeing him in a certain role, such as the one who makes the money. Remember how you were first attracted to him by how handsome he was. Similar to what he has done in seeking objectification in women, you may also have objectified.

The point is for both of you to get beyond any fantasies of how you'd like each other to be and live in the truth of who you both are. That's where ultimate beauty is found.

Exercise: Seeing Behind the Mask

Every one of us presents an image to the world, to ourselves, and to those around us. It is natural to show the pleasing aspects of ourselves and more difficult to show the facets that we feel are ugly or bad. This exercise, meant for both partners, helps you see behind the mask, and to take the first step toward moving past objectification.

First, you need to (if possible) find three pictures of yourself—one when you were a young child, one when you were a teenager, and one of yourself now. If you can't find these three photos, find whatever photos you can. Please don't let a lack of photos keep you from doing the exercise; whatever you can put together will work.

Step One

You will need your three photos and a mirror. Any mirror will do, even the bathroom mirror. The mirror just has to be large enough so that you can see your entire face. Find some quiet time when you can be uninterrupted for ten to fifteen minutes.

Sit down and look at your three photos. Pay close attention to the eyes in the photos. Spend three or four minutes looking at each photo. Notice how you may judge the characteristics of your form, the way you smile, the tilt of your eyes, the color of your hair. Notice how you may judge whatever you personally perceive to be a flaw or what you perceive to be an asset.

Then drop those perceptions as much as you can and just notice who is looking out of the eyes in the photo. Who is there? What is the quality or essence of that individual? Do this with each of the photos, taking several minutes with each.

Then go to the mirror and examine your reflection. Look into your own eyes. Again, notice how you may judge whatever you personally perceive to be a flaw or an asset. Then drop that perception or judgment and notice, really see, who is looking out of your eyes. What or who do you see looking back at you that is the same or different from what you saw looking out of the eyes in the photos? Spend a minute or two just investigating what you may perceive.

Step Two

Next, exchange photos with your partner. You can do this step immediately after you have done step one or at a different time. If you and your partner are too angry or hurt by each other at this time, please postpone step two until you feel ready to do it. It is better to postpone than to do something that you feel will create more distance. Trust yourself in knowing the right time to complete this exercise. When you are ready, be sure that you have fifteen to twenty minutes available and that both you and your partner can do this part of the exercise together.

As you did with your own photos, look at each of the photos of your partner one at a time. Spend three or four minutes looking at each photo. Pay close attention to the eyes in the photos. Notice how you may judge the characteristics of your partner's form, the way he or she smiles, the tilt of the eyes, the hair color. Notice how you may judge whatever you perceive to be a flaw or an asset to your partner's looks. Then drop those perceptions as much as you can and just notice who is looking out of the eyes in the photo. Who is there? Do this with each of the photos for several minutes.

Next, sit down directly across from your partner. Look directly into your partner's eyes. Notice how you may judge whatever you perceive to be a flaw or an asset. Then drop that perception or judgment and look and see who is looking out of your partner's eyes. What or who do you see looking back at you that is the same as or different from what you saw looking out of the eyes in the photos? Spend a minute or two just investigating what you see.

Finally, spend a few minutes discussing whatever you have experienced with your partner. The next time you feel angry or hurt by your partner, bring to mind, as much as you can, the young child, the teenager, and the vulnerable adult that you have seen in your partner's eyes. And as much as possible, allow yourself to remember the innocent young child, the teenager, and the vulnerable adult that you have experienced by looking into your own eyes. Who is it that is behind that mask?

CHAPTER SUMMARY

- The sexual connection with someone you feel deeply connected to is powerful yet vulnerable. When an issue with sexual compulsivity is thrown into that already powerful yet vulnerable mix, a potentially explosive situation occurs.
- Whatever your reaction may be to discovering (or being discovered with) sexually addictive behaviors, you will be able to survive the reactions and shock of this time.
- The partner who has been sexually compulsive needs to have the desire and willingness to stop sexually acting out. The partner who has been betrayed needs to have the desire and willingness to go through the process of investigation with her partner. Both partners also need to be willing to begin to look into the dynamics within the relationship system that are not working.
- Moving through the blockages to intimacy that are revealed through the healing of your partnership can bring your relationship back from what may appear to be certain disaster.

Looking Forward

In Chapter 3, we will begin to look at how sexual addiction or compulsion shows up in relationships, and how couples have been able to use this troubling issue and difficult time to find ways to deepen their relationship with themselves and with each other.

CHAPTER 3

Sex Addiction and Your Relationship

Being in a relationship is difficult. To greater and lesser degrees, we all have our challenges in learning to play in the sandbox with each other. Inside a relationship, we can use our commitment to each other as a holding vessel that allows each of us to heal whatever is preventing the intimacy we deeply desire. Each person in the relationship can, if willing, uncover the individual and joint blockages to true partnership. The commitment, the connection, the love, the container of the relationship can support each partner in being able to see what is standing in the way of greater intimacy.

We would like to stress again that before you can move forward with your relationship, the partner who has been sexually compulsive needs to have the desire and willingness to stop sexually acting out. If the desire and willingness to stop is not in place, then you don't have a basis from which to begin.

Additionally, the partner who has been betrayed needs to have the desire and willingness to go through the process of investigation with her partner. Both partners also need to be willing to begin to look into the dynamics within the relationship system that are not working. What is preventing true intimacy? How is each partner contributing to the difficulties in the relationship?

Why Is This Problem in My Relationship?

We recently heard a country song that stated that if you aren't getting "good loving" at home, find your loving somewhere else. This is exactly the distorted logic that can drive someone to attempt to find relief in a way that only exacerbates the problem. We recognize that it can feel like the path of least resistance is to view porn and masturbate or to seek another warm body to find the relief and connectedness you desire. The problem is that if you try to deal with your issues outside of your committed relationship, the issue will never be resolved. You will only drive your problem deeper, and you will not be able to find the relief and closeness you are actually seeking.

The urges to connect sexually and to experience pleasure in the waves of orgasm are natural. In an ideal world, we would be able to retain our innocence around our sexuality. Ideally, our pubescent sexuality would lead us to the connected, loving, and intimate connection that is possible in human coupling. But outside of this idealized perfect potentiality, we have the opportunity and challenge in our closest relationships to come face to face with the wounding around our sexuality that occurred in our childhood years and/or as we moved through pubescence. We can find our way to a healthy sexual connection.

We tend to be surprised when sexuality and/or intimacy become issues in our close partnerships. But where else would the issues and difficulties we might have around sexuality and intimacy arise? Our closest relationships are exactly the place offering us the opportunity to heal the wounds that may have moved us away from the naturalness of our sexual expression and/or away from our natural connectedness with others. Our relationships offer the forum to work with and heal the ways in which we have difficulty with attachment, connection, bonding, and commitment.

Level 1 Sexual Addiction

In this book, we are only able to deal with what have been called Level 1 sex addictions. This includes behaviors that, while unacceptable inside committed relationships, are more widely accepted by society: viewing porn, masturbating, visiting chat rooms, hiring prostitutes, and compulsive brief or long-term affairs and relationships.

Behaviors that involve more serious legal consequences, such as exhibitionism and voyeurism, are beyond the scope of this book, as are behaviors that cause serious consequences for the victims, including incest, child molestation, and rape.

If either you or your partner is involved in behaviors beyond Level 1, we urge you to seek professional help and support. Chapter 11 includes resources for seeking such support.

Level 1 Behaviors In-Depth

We have found that Level 1 sex addiction or compulsivity can manifest in layers (or types). One layer is not necessarily separate from another layer. The layers are not necessarily progressive; each type of behavior can reinforce or lead to another.

The most common form of sexual compulsivity that we see today is one partner getting hooked on viewing Internet porn and then masturbating. However, the layers or types of Level 1 behaviors may include:

- Sexually compulsive activities within the relationship including sex that is not coupled with respect for the needs and desires of the other partner, such as using the partner as a sex object
- Lack of ability to engage in sexual contact with one's partner
- Sexual fantasy, viewing pornography, and masturbation (no contact with actual live people)
- Visiting chat rooms or online sexual live feeds or posing as a single person on online dating sites—contact with live people, but no physical contact

- Engaging sexually with live people but without emotional connection—including contact with prostitutes, massage parlors, emotionless dating, and affairs
- Engaging sexually with live people with an emotional connection—including brief or long-term relationships and affairs

These layers may, of course, overlap and merge with each other. An individual can be engaged at different times in any number of these layers. We list them to help you see that you or your partner are not the only people to be impacted by sexually compulsive behaviors. These are patterns that impact many others as well—you are not alone.

Sexually Compulsive Behavior Inside the Relationship

Even in a relationship that is generally working smoothly, one or both partners can easily lose track of the individuality of the other partner. At times, it can be difficult to remember that your partner views and experiences life through an entirely different lens. We want what we want when we want it, sometimes regardless of what our partner wants. And that "when we want it" is often right now. The urge of the sexual drive combined with the vulnerability, privacy, and tenderness of the sexual connection can cause one partner to mindlessly run over the other partner without realizing what he or she is doing.

We have seen that it is possible that neither partner is fully cognizant of this type of betrayal. There can be a demand or a perceived need for sex from one's partner that is not coupled with respect for the partner's needs and boundaries. For example, one partner may demand a type of sexual activity with which their partner does not feel comfortable. Often, one partner may go along with the request of the other out of a sense of obligation, duty, or out of a fear of loss of love or financial support.

One husband believed he couldn't go to sleep if he didn't have sex with his wife each night. His wife went along with him because she was afraid he would have an affair if she didn't. Another husband, a quite successful stock portfolio manager, demanded sex with his wife any day the market declined 100 points or more. This husband didn't realize his sexual needs were tied to the stock market, but his wife did.

We have found that, at times, a heterosexual man will have fantasies and desires about having anal intercourse with his partner. We have also found that it is quite common for the woman to find this type of sexual contact not only unsatisfying but also thoroughly unappealing, even though she may have been willing to give it a try. This again is a situation where we encourage women to honor their feelings, their bodies, themselves. This is not to say that some women may find this type of sexual contact satisfying. The point is that we encourage men and women alike to honor their feelings and their bodies as well as their partners' feelings and bodies.

Marie and Jim

Marie had been married to Jim for a little more than twenty years. Jim was a very successful real estate developer and Marie was a writer and stay-at-home mom until their three daughters left for college. Jim called us to seek help for his compulsion with masturbating to Internet porn. Because of the porn Jim had been viewing, he had begun taking videos when he had sex with Marie. Marie was never comfortable with this activity, but went along with Jim because she thought that if he were taking videos of the two of them together then he would at least be having sex with her and not with the pictures on the Internet.

As Marie began to tell the truth about her lack of comfort around the videos, she was able to tell Jim she didn't want to do it anymore. Marie was concerned that if she didn't go along with Jim she would lose their sex life altogether. However, in time, the truth-telling Marie did about her discomfort with the videos enabled Jim to understand how he actually needed to connect with his wife if they were going to have an intimate relationship. This, in turn, helped Jim become motivated to address his compulsion with viewing porn.

Lack of Ability to Connect Sexually with Your Partner

Sexual addiction can also manifest as the inability for the sexually compulsive individual to engage sexually with his partner. He only feels safe with sexual activity that does not require actual intimate connection. This is more common than you might imagine.

For some, being with a real person can feel too intimate and scary. An individual may only feel safe in expressing himself sexually through masturbation to images or he may only feel safe in engaging in sex with a prostitute. It is a sad truth that men who have been abused in some way are prone to finding sex with their partner frightening or distasteful. Intimate sexual contact has become distorted, or the excitement of sex with someone perpetually new or different is the only way an individual knows how to express himself sexually.

One of the common themes we see is that of the son who became his mother's "little man." At the heart of this dynamic, the mother turns to her son as her partner, often without recognizing what she is doing. He becomes her hero. When that little boy grows up and recognizes that same motherly love coming from his partner, he begins to lose his desire to have sex with his partner. He often does not recognize that this has happened, but his wife has suddenly moved from sex partner to mother. This could happen when he witnesses her with their child or even through the act of her preparing meals and serving them. He sees his partner in the role of mother, and is catapulted into the territory of relating to mother.

Pornography can seem the perfect solution because he can search for images that look like women he was attracted to when he was awakening sexually. We have seen men search for porn images or prostitutes who replicate a particular person—someone who fits the image of the person with whom he was first involved.

At times, men begin using porn and masturbating because the sexual connection inside their relationship has temporarily lessened—for example when children arrive on the scene or maybe when their partner has become engrossed in work or in a project. We would call this type of flare-up of masturbating using pornography episodic rather than chronic. This does not mean that the compulsion to continue using the pornography as a sexual outlet rather than connecting with their partner is any less overwhelming. However, we have found that this kind of fixation is easier to work with than one that is more deeply ingrained or has been in place for a longer period of time.

Linda and Tom

Tom's way of coping with the frustrations in his life was to go to men's clubs. As he got older, he wanted to settle down and wooed a very sexy dancer from one of the clubs. They had a fantastic sexual relationship until Linda got pregnant. Then, for Tom, Linda moved into the category of mom, which meant he could no longer be attracted. Growing up, Tom had seen his father seek women outside the marriage, and that was his model. As a result, Tom had grown up in a household without real connection and had no models of intimacy on which to base his behavior. Tom knew something was missing, and he had always felt less than some of his friends who were able to maintain "normal" relationships. Yet here he was, married, no longer wanting to have sex with his wife, and going back to men's clubs in search of lap dances and possible sexual partners.

Linda had also grown up in a household lacking in intimacy and in which the men made sexualizing and objectifying remarks about the women. By the time she was a teenager, the behavior she was most familiar with was being seen as an object.

In counseling, Linda and Tom were both able to discover and identify the way they saw themselves and what they expected in sexual relationships. Although it was not an easy or comfortable task, both were ultimately able to break from their past associations and forge a new and more intimate relationship with each other.

Sexually Compulsive Behavior Using Pornography

Men who act out sexually by viewing pornography and masturbating never get enough to be satisfied for long. They may or may not have regular sex with their partners, but usually become more attached to the fantasy than the reality of sexual contact with a real person. Therefore, their close relationships are lacking in intimacy.

Some sex addicts pose as single men on dating sites, where they interact with live people, but again, this is not real intimate contact. Even when a man relates to a woman via a chat line or the Internet it is not a real encounter. There are also men who pose as women in online chat rooms so they will be sexually degraded by other men. All of these situations are based on fantasy and are fake, such as when the man is pretending to be single or the woman is being paid to act interested in the man.

Josh and Lisa

It was two in the morning and Josh was wide awake, lying in bed next to his beautiful young wife. As usual, he was torturing himself with memories of preteen sexual encounters and the guilt he felt about them. Seeking relief from the thoughts, Josh quietly slipped out of bed and went down the hallway to a guest room, where his laptop was set up.

As he had done almost every night for months, Josh logged into an Internet site and found a woman he wanted. She was live on the Internet and the site was set up so that Josh paid the website company and could tell the woman to do whatever he wanted—up to a point. There were certain acts that cost more to see. Men who frequent such sites typically masturbate while telling the women how and when to take off their clothes and how and when to move their bodies. Josh began by asking the woman to remove her blouse. He had been to similar sites for years, but thought he could stop after marrying Lisa. Like many men, he kept telling himself that he would just do it one more time.

Lisa woke up briefly and realized that Josh was not in the bed. She glanced toward the bathroom, but it was empty. Then she noticed a flickering light down the hallway. They had only been married for six months, but their sexual contact had diminished, and Lisa had not pushed Josh for more. Although she suspected something was troubling Josh, he had assured Lisa that it wasn't her. Although it was true that she was not the source of the problem, and although he loved her, Josh was not able to be vulnerable with her by telling her what he thought of as his darkest secrets—secrets which were in the way of their marital intimacy.

Standing quietly at the door to the guest room, Lisa could see the naked woman on the laptop computer's screen. Although Josh's back was to her, she knew what he was doing. Sensing Lisa's presence, Josh glanced back, saw her, and slammed the laptop closed. But it was too late. His secret was out, or at least part of it.

Shaking her head, Lisa turned away, ran back to their bedroom, and slammed and locked the door. Josh begged her to let him explain. He pleaded that he would tell her the truth. At first, Lisa would not listen. Finally, she opened the door and Josh cringed at her tear-streaked face. He thought he had shattered their love forever. "Let's talk in the kitchen," she said.

They made coffee and sat at the kitchen table. Lisa had known a few crucial facts about Josh's childhood. Josh's father was an angry alcoholic, frequently at the local bar, and Josh's mother was not around much, either. This gave Josh plenty of time alone in the house, with only his little brother at home now and then. Lisa also knew that Josh had been teased at school and often felt like an outsider.

Now Josh haltingly told her that when he was ten years old, he and a friend began playing around sexually—and the friend was another boy. One day, Josh's little brother came home and found the two older boys naked and engaging in oral sex. Josh allowed his younger brother to participate, which Josh believed later caused great emotional distress for his younger brother, who had difficulty maintaining any type of relationship. Lisa saw the shame on Josh's face and knew this must be what had been torturing him. But there was more.

Josh felt even worse about what happened when a ten-year-old neighbor girl spied on Josh and his friend during a sexual encounter. She wanted to know what they were doing or she would tell. The neighbor girl followed Josh's instructions to lie down. He clumsily climbed on top and began to "dry hump" her. Terrified, the girl pushed him off and ran back to her house. The neighbor girl stopped speaking to Josh, and about two months later, she and her family moved to another town.

Josh began crying. He feared that by telling Lisa the truth, she would condemn him as he had been condemning himself for all these years and he would lose her forever. But Josh's honesty and vulnerability were having the opposite effect on Lisa. She felt closer to Josh. Yet, she also knew that their marriage had real problems.

In counseling, they gradually understood how, because of the situation with Josh's parents and his early sexual encounters, he had no grounding in how to have a truly intimate relationship with a woman. He loved Lisa, but had unresolved shame that was in the way of allowing himself to be with a real woman. Lisa also examined how she was brought up with alcoholic parents and saw her own fears of intimacy. It took many months, but together they were able to learn to be vulnerable and how to take concrete steps toward a more intimate relationship. They both faced the shame and pain they felt around intimacy, including sex. Rather than punishing him for his past behavior, Lisa took steps to initiate frequent lovemaking with Josh, and they began to enjoy each other more than either ever thought possible.

Sexually Compulsive Behavior with a Real Person

This type of sexually compulsive behavior includes contact with prostitutes, emotionless dating, and affairs that are more sexual than emotional. Because this behavior requires contact outside the boundaries of a marriage, the consequences can be more severe than some other types of behaviors. As has been mentioned before, the first step toward recovery is for the acting-out partner to completely stop his sexually compulsive behavior. Then, if both partners are committed to stopping blame and shame and to examining the root causes of their own behaviors as well as the foundations of their relationship, they are often able to not only keep the marriage but to reach a new and more satisfying level of closeness, connection, and intimacy.

Tanya and Brandon

Brandon engaged in addictive behavior long before he met and married Tanya. While they were dating, he overcame his drug and alcohol addiction, but he still had a gambling addiction and, unbeknownst to her, a sex addiction. At times of stress in his life, such as when a relationship was not going well, Brandon's addictive behavior would become almost completely out of control.

As a child, Brandon would hide until his parents were frantic to find him. He craved attention, and negative attention was better than none at all. Brandon grew up with an angry alcoholic father and, rather than intimacy, what he saw between his parents was warfare and mistrust. Brandon's concept of a relationship was that he needed to be on guard, and he was quick to argue or attack.

Tanya grew up in a family in which her father was a good provider but distant. Although this is a simplified view of what was a complex set of factors, on one level Tanya craved love from a distant man. Brandon fit the bill perfectly: He was a very successful stockbroker and although he felt love for Tanya, it was difficult for him to express himself or be romantic.

Even after five years of marriage, Tanya was not sure how much Brandon loved or trusted her. Although she knew about his drug and alcohol addictions, she suspected he had others. However, she was afraid that if she confronted Brandon, he would leave her. Only when she began examining the family finances did she realize that Brandon had spent over $50,000 in one year at massage parlors and with prostitutes. She knew if their marriage was to survive, they needed to start being honest and face their problems.

After they started counseling, Brandon agreed to stop acting out sexually. But if he sensed the mood of the relationship was uncertain or that Tanya was pushing him too much to change, he would feel a strong need to stop at a massage parlor. Brandon would go inside, pay, accompany a woman to a room, but then stop himself from going further and leave. Although Brandon's behavior still angered Tanya, Brandon felt he had taken steps to break his addiction. Yet Tanya and Brandon both knew the truth. If the relationship got too difficult and Brandon was too uncomfortable with being emotionally vulnerable, he could resort to acting out sexually. If this couple was to achieve lasting intimacy, they had much more emotional work to do, on themselves and the relationship.

Sexual Encounters with an Emotional Component

Sexually compulsive behavior can include brief or long-term relationships or affairs with an emotional connection. These usually secret relationships occur outside the primary relationship. The person having such affairs may be seeking an intimacy he is not getting within the primary love relationship. Another reason is that the man's view of his wife as sexual has shifted to one that is more maternal. As mentioned, this can occur after the woman has become pregnant, has children, or is even just regularly cooking for him as his own mother once did. Sometimes the man's relationship with his mother in childhood was one where she acted inappropriately toward him and, for example, tried to treat him as an equal or a surrogate husband, rather than as her child. Such behavior by the mother frequently indicated a lack of intimacy between the mother and father, which meant the child did not learn to be intimate in a healthy way.

Barbara and Christopher

In the early stages of their relationship, Barbara and Christopher had an intense sexual and emotional charge. In fact, they forged a bond that they would never part. While Barbara pursued a degree in internal medicine, Christopher financially supported them both by teaching art history at a local university.

Because Barbara's career path meant spending many hours studying and at classes, Christopher had a lot of time to himself. He had grown up with a mother who was raising five children and barely had enough time to attend to them all or her husband. As a boy, Christopher decided that he had to fend for himself, and when he was in his teens, saw his father as a model for finding sex and companionship either in or out of the primary love relationship. As a result, Christopher had always felt entitled to satisfying his sexual desires.

Early in his relationship with Barbara, she was the source of his satisfaction. But when Barbara's career path took most of her time and energy, Christopher began to feel neglected. After finishing her medical residency, Barbara joined a group of other doctors practicing internal medicine. She quickly became a favorite of patients due to her unusually compassionate and attentive way of relating. She was, in fact, giving to her patients what Christopher had been craving.

In addition, as Barbara's career and income took off, she began to attempt to "help" Christopher by needling him about his lack of career advancement, about his being content to teach art history. She was the doctor who "fixed" people, and she related to Christopher almost as if he was another patient who needed fixing so he could live his life in what she thought was a better way.

That's when cute, twenty-year-old Caitlin became a front-row center admiring student in Christopher's art history class. Although Christopher had previously briefly dallied with several students, Caitlin was different. Although he still loved Barbara and wanted a loving relationship with her, he fell in love with Caitlin. Christopher might have approached Barbara and told her how he was feeling, but he could not allow himself to be that vulnerable. As is the case with many men, it was easier for him to seek satisfaction outside the relationship. He thought he could just love both women, while having his sexual desires satisfied with Caitlin. However, because this time Christopher had fallen in love, Barbara ultimately realized that her marriage was in jeopardy. Christopher's realization was that the most important pact in his life was not with Caitlin, but with Barbara.

The couple sought counseling. Barbara came to grips with the fact that she was not being a true partner to her husband. Christopher worked on resolving issues that he had carried around since childhood. They both began to face the truth of their marriage.

What Is "Normal" Sex and Intimacy

In addition to formal marriage contracts, most relationships have either spoken or unspoken agreements about what each person "signed up for" in the relationship and what behavior is acceptable or not. For example, some wives who have little interest in sex have an unspoken agreement that their husbands can seek sexual satisfaction elsewhere. Such relationships typically preclude true intimacy and are not what this book is about. But what behavior does qualify a marriage as having a healthy and positive sexual relationship?

Although there may be no such thing as "normal" sex and intimacy, there are certain clues or guidelines that a relationship is healthy and positive. You can be in an intimate relationship that is not sexual. You can love another person and not be sexual. But most close relationships that are nonsexual could be more accurately categorized as intimate friendships. What makes the marital relationship so special, and affords it the opportunity for a unique intimacy that exists nowhere else in your life, is when the marital partners have sex—and only with each other. Such relationships can exist without sex, particularly when couples are very advanced in age and neither partner wants nor needs sexual interaction. Again, you can also love someone and not engage in sexual behavior. However, a marital relationship where one partner wants a sexual connection that does not exist frequently results in an imbalanced relationship and a barrier to intimacy.

One intent of this book is to help you remove blame, shame, and pain barriers to achieving intimacy. As a couple, you may be able to take steps toward this end on your own. It's also important to realize that you may ultimately also require more intensive counseling practices than a book can provide. In Chapter 11, we offer resources for finding additional help if that is what you feel you may need.

Exercise: Finding a Way to Communicate

It may not seem like it at first, but there is great relief in finally bringing secrets into the light. The following exercise will provide a pathway toward admitting such secrets to your partner. Even though just one of you has been acting out sexually, we can assume that both of you are experiencing a lack of intimacy or closeness in your relationship, and that both of you would like to find a way to feel closer or more intimate with each other.

The first step in building intimacy with your partner is understanding your part in what is happening in the relationship. To do that, you need to see and admit to yourself what your role in the dance has been.

First, make a list (just for yourself) of everything that you suspect is standing in the way of the intimacy that you would like to have with your partner. This is not a list of what your partner is doing to block intimacy; this is a list of what is happening within you. You will keep this list private. Later, you will be able to choose if you would like to share what you have written and, if so, which parts you would like to share. For now, this list is just for you. You are creating it to build an inventory of information for yourself. This is not a list of ammunition to be used to make you or your partner feel wrong or bad. The goal is to create a list for yourself of what you are doing that is preventing closeness and intimacy with your partner.

If you don't feel comfortable writing or working solo, this exercise can also be done with a trusted friend. At this point, we find it is better if you do not do this exercise with your partner. If you do work with a friend, ask the friend to not counsel you or give you advice or feedback. Your friend's job in this exercise will be to simply ask the questions and allow you to find your answers. Your assisting friend might ask supporting questions like, "Tell me more" or "What else do you know about that?"

Whether you write your answers or speak them with your trusted friend, as you investigate, don't just stop with your first response or the most obvious answer. You will gain the most from the exercise if you can let yourself not know the facts as you have always known them. Let yourself be surprised by how you answer, as if you'd never thought about or heard the question before.

Questions for Him

We know you may be looking at some behaviors that you don't like and don't want to admit. That's okay. This is the time to think like a scientist and investigate as dispassionately as possible exactly what you have been doing. You don't need to answer every question. The questions below are only here to get you started.

- How have you acted out sexually? Start with the worst of it. Just write it down. Take your time. Follow the thread of your compulsive behavior.
- Are there any other ways that you acted out sexually?
- What else is a part of your sexually acting-out behavior?
- What triggers your sexually acting-out behaviors or thoughts? What is happening, what are you thinking before your sexual acting out starts?
- Where does your sexual acting-out behavior begin? Is there a pattern? For example, are you sitting at your computer, at the mall, at work feeling bored or trying to solve a difficult problem?

- Do you have any repeating fantasies or thoughts about acting out sexually?
- How do you attempt to hide or mask your problem from others?
- How do you sexualize and objectify?
- How did you relate to your sexuality when you first discovered masturbation?
- How about when you first made sexual contact with another person?
- Have you really wanted to be in this relationship?
- What has kept you here?
- Have you been feeling distant from your partner?
- Have you been distracted?
- Have you put up barriers consciously or unconsciously?
- What has been happening for you in your relationship? What is your overall experience of your relationship with your partner?
- How have you not expressed yourself in this relationship?

Sit down on multiple occasions if you need to, and give yourself permission to recall every way you can remember that you compulsively get on the train and ride it to achieving a momentary orgasmic release. Give creating this list the same kind of time and attention you have given to your compulsive sexual behaviors. In time, creating this list will have a reward for you that those sexual behaviors never did. Revealing to yourself what you have done, really admitting it to yourself, is a key to your liberation. Go for it.

Questions for Her

We know you are in a tough spot. This is hard. In this moment, just for this part of your investigation, we'd like you to actually not think about or focus on what your partner has been doing or how he has been unavailable to you. His part of the exercise will assist him in looking at what he has been doing. We are interested in what has been going on for you.

We would also like you to think as a scientist and investigate as dispassionately as possible exactly what you have been doing. There may be some very good reasons you have not been entirely engaged in this relationship, but it is likely that you have not been fully participating with your partner. Below are questions to help you investigate the particular ways that you keep yourself separate, protected, and thus not truly vulnerable and intimately connected with your partner. You don't need to answer every question. The questions are only here to get you started.

- What has been happening for you in your relationship? What is your overall experience of your relationship with your partner?
- How have you not expressed yourself in this relationship?
- What has been getting in the way of your wanting to be with him?
- What's been preoccupying you?
- How have you been short-changing yourself?
- What did you notice and not pay attention to? What did you see and dismiss about your partner's sexually acting out or about ways that your relationship is unfulfilling to you?
- Have you been sexually frustrated?
- Did you think that this was just how a relationship works?
- Have you believed that it is possible to actually connect intimately with another person without selling yourself out or manipulating?
- What, if anything, has prevented you from expressing your deeply felt needs, or even allowing yourself to have them?

- What has prevented you from feeling that you can be fully intimate?
- What has been getting in the way of your wanting to be with your partner?
- Have you really wanted to be in this relationship?
- What has kept you here?
- Have you been feeling distant from your partner?
- Have you been distracted?
- Have you put up barriers consciously or unconsciously?

Sit down on multiple occasions if you need to and give yourself permission to recall all the ways that you have distanced yourself from your partner or ignored his distance from you. Revealing to yourself what you see, really admitting it to yourself, is a key to your liberation. Go for it.

For Both—If You Choose to Share

The list of information you have created is for you. You may choose to share some of it, all of it, or none of it with your partner. Full disclosure will be important, but you may not be ready for that just yet. At the end of Chapter 4, we discuss creating a space and the ground rules for full disclosure by the partner who has been acting sexually compulsively.

For now, it is important that you find a way to communicate without further distancing yourself from your partner. We have found that it is useful to have some ground rules.

Ground Rules for Communicating Difficult Issues

It is up to each of you to find a way to keep your conversation focused on the issue at hand, to speak fully, and to listen fully. We recognize how difficult these conversations can be, but we also know how they can be a time of opening.

1. First, plan ahead—make an appointment with each other. Be sure you have time and space where you will not be interrupted. Allow as much time as you think you will need. You can schedule separate times for each of you to talk, if you feel that will work the best for you. We have found that you will probably each need at least half an hour to speak.
2. Secondly, in each of your sessions, the person who is listening says nothing until the other person is finished speaking. This might take five minutes or fifteen minutes or longer. The speaker has the floor. When the speaker is finished talking, the listener becomes the speaker and can reply without interruption. The important ingredient is that the speaker knows that he or she can speak until finished. The process of speaking and then replying can be repeated as many times as is necessary within each sharing session. Remember, these sessions are not for finding solutions, but simply for being heard, for getting things out on the table.
3. Remember, the goal of the listener is to be quiet and let the speaker talk. This will pay off. While the listener may feel a strong urge to defend or make excuses, this is not necessary. Now is simply a time to listen. Listening without defending is the beginning of a new level of communication in your relationship.
4. For each speaker, remember to speak to the action and to the feeling. Don't demean the other's character. Hurtful things have been done (maybe by each of you), but this does not make the person who did them inherently bad or unredeemable. It is not your job to try to fix or diagnose your partner. Just speak

about your experience—how you are feeling. When it is your turn to be the listener, simply listen. If you feel defensive or angry, take some deep breaths. Remind yourself that you are receiving information, not ammunition.

5. Finally, at the end of the sessions, each partner needs to say one thing they appreciate about the other. Don't attempt to be extra generous by telling more than one thing, but do think of one thing that you truly appreciate. Then thank your partner for being honest and willing to have this difficult conversation. And then, either silently or openly, thank yourself for your honesty and willingness. Having this kind of conversation shows great strength of character.

Once you have recognized and admitted to yourself that there is a problem and have started to gain some understanding of the nature of the problem, you can begin to build deeper intimacy, love, and connectedness.

CHAPTER SUMMARY

- Being in a relationship is difficult, but if you deal with the difficulty outside of the committed relationship, the issue will never be resolved. You only drive the problem deeper rather than finding the relief and intimate closeness that you are seeking.

Level 1 sexually addictive behaviors may include:

1. Sexually compulsive activities within the relationship including sex that is not coupled with respect for the needs and desires of the other partner, such as using the partner as a sex object

2. Lack of ability to engage in sexual contact with one's partner
3. Sexual fantasy, viewing pornography, and masturbation (no contact with actual live people)
4. Visiting chat rooms or online sexual live feeds or posing as a single person on online dating sites—contact with live people, but no actual physical contact
5. Engaging sexually with live people but without emotional connection—including contact with prostitutes, massage parlors, emotionless dating, and affairs
6. Engaging sexually with live people with an emotional connection—including brief or long-term relationships and affairs

- Although there may be no such thing as "normal" sex and intimacy, there are certain clues or guidelines that a relationship is healthy and positive. What makes the marital relationship so special, and affords it the opportunity for a unique intimacy that exists nowhere else in your life, is when the marital partners have sex—and only with each other.

Looking Forward

At the end of Chapter 4, you will find guidelines for full disclosure. Prior to that, we provide some clarity about many of the misperceptions you may be having about yourself or your partner.

CHAPTER 4

What Does This Mean about You?

Whatever the particular type of sexually compulsive behavior that is intruding into your relationship, certain patterns of thought can be obstacles to moving forward effectively. No matter what side of this problem you are on, there are some familiar themes.

Generally, women want to know what their partners' behaviors mean about them and about their relationship. And women often want to know what they can do to help their partners. They would like to somehow ensure that the problem will not happen again.

Usually, men are ashamed about what they have been doing, while at the same time they often attempt to minimize the problem. Men can also have a tendency to blame their partners, their biology, and/or the society in which they live.

To illustrate, let's look at Heather and Bryan's story from an e-mail Heather sent to us.

Heather and Bryan

My name is Heather and I am in need of some serious advice. I just don't know who to turn to about this issue. I am twenty years old and I live with my twenty-one-year-old boyfriend, Bryan. We are absolutely head over heels in love and spend most of our time together. About six months ago, I discovered that Bryan had a secret problem that he was keeping to himself. I think he might be addicted to Internet porn.

After I first discovered the numerous porn sites on his computer, I was devastated. I thought, "Am I not enough?" I can't live up to the intense, airbrushed, perfect women on those sites. I freaked out, and as he calmed me down, he told me he didn't have a problem, that he's just a guy and it was an occasional thing.

Shortly after that, a few days later, I found even more porn on his computer. I was devastated even more. He had initially led me to believe that his using porn was occasional. After that second time I caught him, he finally told me that he had been dealing with his problem with Internet porn since the age of twelve. At that time, he had his own computer and it was just an easy click to see whatever he wanted.

He reassured me that it had nothing to do with being unsatisfied with me or with my body. It was an impulse, an urge. After that, he swore he would never look at the porn again, that I meant too much to him to lose me over it. He promised that if he did, he would tell me.

So for about a month and a half, as far as I know, he didn't look at anything. But then last Thursday I used his phone to get on the Internet, and right there were a couple of sites he had visited on his break at work. At work! Of course, I was absolutely heartbroken again. I went straight to him and asked, "What the hell is this?" He apologized profusely and said, "I swear, I really don't look at that stuff anymore. I was just at work and I don't even know why I did it, I'm so sorry." He then told me that he thought it would be too hard to tell me that he had looked at porn again because he knew I would get upset. I told him, "I am upset, but it's always something we can still work through."

The problem is that I gave Bryan my trust twice already, and he abused it. Now this time he assures me that he doesn't have a problem with porn anymore—I have nothing to worry about. But I do worry. I worry constantly that he'll have a "slip up" and look just once more, and then just once more, etc., and not tell me about it.

I have read a lot about sexual addiction and addiction to Internet porn, and Bryan shows all the signs of having an addiction. He told me he still has urges all the time to look, but fights it. He tried to hide it from me because he was embarrassed he couldn't stop. He even looked at it on his work break because he thought he would be able to just look at a couple of pictures and be good and that I wouldn't find out.

I worry that until he admits to having an addiction, he won't truly be able to stop. He needs to realize that he needs to do this for himself. He tells me that he doesn't like that he looks at the porn and he feels ashamed after he does. He knows how I feel about it, so the only way I can understand his problem is that it is an addiction. But he hates that word and assures me he doesn't have a problem anymore—let alone an addiction—and that I have nothing to worry about. How can I show him that his problem is way more serious than he thinks it is? How can I sort this thing out?

Thanks for your help,

Heather

From Heather's e-mail, we can be certain that each partner in the relationship has issues and that the relationship between them needs help. However, it seems that Heather and Bryan have reached conclusions that are just not accurate. Let's start with the reassurances we would give to both Heather and Bryan—and to you.

Keep in mind that we offer these reassurances knowing that they are important to hear, but also realizing that they are not going to solve the problem. They probably will not penetrate to the core of the internal machinery that has created the problem. We will follow up in later chapters with tools to unravel the mechanisms that are contributing to the difficulty you are experiencing inside yourself and with your partner. We will show you how to work with the underlying motivating causes. In the meantime, think of these reassurances as seeds that are being planted, and take in these reassurances as deeply as you can. We also strongly recommend that you read through the reassurances for both you and for your partner. Understanding the issue from your significant other's point of view is vital to your development of compassion and empathy.

For Her: What This Does Not Mean about You

As we mentioned in Chapter 1, you should know that you did not cause your partner's sexually compulsive behavior, nor can you cure it. That will be his task. His behavior is not about you. It certainly affects you, but it is not due to anything you have done or not done. His sexually compulsive behavior was in place before you met him. You may be (and probably are) an irritant and a stimulant to him at varying times, but his choices about how to deal with his irritations and stimulations are his alone, as are yours.

His fixation with sexuality outside of your relationship does not mean that he does not love you. In our experience, men who are fixated sexually with images or even with people outside of their relationship can still deeply love their partners. They just don't know how to connect intimately and sexually, even though they truly love their partners and want to have a real intimate relationship. Clearly, your relationship is not hopeless or doomed because your partner has a problem with sexual compulsivity.

You need to put in place several important agreements before you can move forward as a couple. Your partner must let you know that he understands he needs to learn how to make other choices in expressing his sexuality. If he is not willing to see that his sexually acting-out behavior is unacceptable in the relationship, then you do not have the ground upon which you can rebuild. He may have no concept of how to work with his sexually compulsive urges at this point, but he must understand that his behaviors have been unacceptable and destructive to your relationship. If your partner is unwilling to 1) recognize that his sexual behaviors are destructive to the relationship, and 2) see that he needs to find a way to alter his repetitive and compulsive tendencies, then your relationship does not have a true chance of moving toward genuine intimacy.

Your partner's fixation with pornographic images or with prostitutes does not mean that you need to compete with the images or the prostitutes. You do not need to turn yourself into a sex object, to fashion yourself into the image of a porn star or sexy prostitute. You would not even want to compete with these images. Your value as a sexual partner is not based on becoming more like the airbrushed illusionary perfection of the plastic world of pornography. When your partner is turned on by and is masturbating to these images, he is not engaged in intimate sex. Alternatively, the sexual connection you are interested in having with your partner is an expression of intimacy.

As we mentioned in Chapter 1, compulsive, addictive sex is not the same thing as intimate sex. Your partner may not understand this yet, but you probably do. You have the capacity to express your beauty, your sexuality, and your love for giving and receiving pleasure with and from your partner. Intimate sex is sacred. It can be fun and playful and intense, but it is not based in compulsion, fear, or shame. It is a powerful expression of loving tenderness born of intimate, vulnerable connection with a loving partner.

You are not weak or damaged just because you want to stay with your partner and rebuild your relationship. You are the judge of what is right for your life, your body, your relationship. However, if your partner is unwilling to admit to his problem with sexual compulsiveness and work toward building the capacity for intimate connected sex, then you need to examine your part in cocreating a relationship that does not honor you as a true partner.

Keep in mind that even if you make a choice that you later determine was an error, it does not necessarily mean that you made a wrong choice for that moment. Sometimes it takes an apparent wrong turn to learn something. Treat yourself as if you are a child learning to walk—you sometimes need to fall down to reach the ultimate goal of being able to dance. If you feel you may be hanging on to your relationship in a compulsive way, we urge you to seek support. In Chapter 11, you will find information on how to learn more about what has been termed co-sex addiction.

You do not have to force yourself to trust your partner right now. Actually, you probably do not trust him now. And you have a good reason for your lack of trust. He has not been faithful to the commitment of the relationship and has probably lied repeatedly. Trust in your relationship will need to be rebuilt. In Chapters 5 and 8, we discuss the rebuilding of trust and the importance of undefended honesty.

You are going to feel angry, upset, and mistrusting. You do not have to banish your reactions; in fact, you can't. In Chapter 7, we show you how you can use the strong feelings and emotions you are having to strengthen your relationship with yourself and your partner. The feelings you are having are normal. Both you and your partner have the task of learning how to tell the truth to yourself and to each other. Through this truth telling, intimacy will be rebuilt and trust will naturally arise. You do not have to force it to come back.

You don't need to do this alone. We have found that in dealing with sexually compulsive behaviors, outside support is frequently necessary. As mentioned, in Chapter 11 you will find information on locating this kind of support. However, this book will provide you with the information and tools you need to begin changing your relationship whether or not you also attend counseling, join a group, or seek other outside support.

Needing support in moving through this process does not mean you are weak. You will need to reach out to connect with friends, family, and other support systems. It is important to find help and comfort that is actually supportive. True support comes from someone who is able to provide real empathy. This does not mean they agree with everything you tell them or having them side with you about how bad and wrong your partner has been. Ideally, you will be able to reveal, to unearth, to expose your story of shame, your story of blame. A compassionate friend will hold a loving space for you to find your own answers. Your support person may point you toward seeing what you cannot see on your own because he or she understands the emotional territory you are traversing, but this person does not force you into that awareness. The key to true support is compassion—for both you and your partner.

For Him: What This Does Not Mean about You

It is common for men who have engaged in sexually compulsive behavior to feel as if they have failed in their relationships with their girlfriends or spouses. But there are sound reasons why you are sexually addicted, and the roots of those motives will be explored in more detail in Chapter 9, which covers your history, or why you behave the way you do.

For now, we want to be clear that being a sex addict does not mean you are a failure. It also does not mean that you are bad or wrong. It does mean that you are living in reaction to your history, which includes the attitudes and role models you saw regarding intimacy while you were growing up, for example.

Because you are reading this book, sexual compulsion is obviously a problem for you and your significant other. Fortunately, it is a problem that can be dealt with, and many men and couples have done just that. We want to be clear that you are not doomed to live with this problem for the rest of your life. You can change.

Firstly, it bears repeating that you can stop acting out sexually. Once you do that, your relationship has a chance to change.

This book explores not just how to move beyond sexually addicted behaviors, but how to achieve a new and more intimate and sexual connection in your relationship. Secondly, you can start being honest with yourself and with your loved one, which can allow more safety and vulnerability into your relationship. The road to vulnerability is paved with undefended honesty, a subject detailed in Chapter 8.

Many men have grown up thinking that all types of sex or sexual connection are basically the same thing—sex. But as mentioned, sex addiction and intimate sex are not the same thing. In fact, they are profoundly different. In Chapter 1, we explained the specifics of our sexual impulses and delineated when sexual activity becomes sexual addiction. For now, it is important that you 1) recognize and admit that you have an issue with sexual compulsivity, and 2) make a commitment to stopping the sexually compulsive behaviors. You may not know how to stop the behaviors, but you can commit to finding a way to stop and to building intimacy with your partner. In fostering your natural vulnerability, you will be able to build true intimacy, including sexual intimacy, with your partner.

Because you have acted out sexually, you may doubt that you love your wife or girlfriend—although, most likely, you do. Being sexually addicted and acting out sexually does not mean you don't love the person you're with; it does mean that you have an issue with intimacy. For example, a real woman has real feelings that you may be uncomfortable with. On the other hand, there is no need for you to deal with reality when you interact with a woman on a porn site or a prostitute or a strip club dancer. That's the fantasy of sexually addictive behavior, and it has no relation to real intimacy.

Although you may have other issues that require psychological counseling, being sexually compulsive does not mean you are mentally ill or sick or crazy. Having engaged in sexually compulsive behavior also does not mean there is something wrong with you or that you are a pervert. Many men feel ashamed of acting out sexually, and they often consider themselves weak. If you feel that way, it does not mean you are weak, but that you have not yet learned how to break free of your sexually compulsive behavior and find true intimacy in your relationship with a loved one.

Most addictive behaviors take you away from what is happening or what you are feeling that you do not know how to deal with in the moment. Chapter 7 provides a deeper understanding of how to deal with strong emotions, vulnerability, and intimacy, along with your responses to hurt, anger, and fear. When you learn to resist the instinctive impulse to get away, you gain the capacity to cope with your emotions in a positive way that can lead to increased honesty and intimacy.

Once you do finally break free of sexually acting out, you understand that by giving up your sexually compulsive behavior you are not losing anything. Quite to the contrary, you are gaining everything. Real intimacy with a real person is worth more than all the money in the world. This book will provide you with methods to determine what is in the way of achieving intimacy with the person you love. Examples of what can be in the way are shame, blame, and pain.

No Magic Bullet

We understand that even though you may hear, understand, and accept the above encouragements, these words will not magically remove your natural responses of anger, fear, and pain. They do not wipe out your underlying story of worthlessness, or remove the pain driven by shame. They will not remove your compulsive urges.

But hearing these reassurances and taking them in is a necessary, important, and helpful step.

Exercise: Disclosure

If you have not already done so, it is time for full disclosure with your partner. If you are not ready to disclose or if you are uncertain about whether or not sexual compulsivity is a problem in your relationship, it may be helpful to reread these first four chapters again. If you feel you need outside support prior to approaching full disclosure, we discuss finding those types of resources in Chapter 11. And it can be helpful to refer back to the "Ground Rules for Communicating Difficult Issues" at the end of Chapter 3.

For Him: The Truth, the Whole Truth

So, the time has come for you to make an appointment with your partner to fill her in on the missing pieces of how your sexual compulsions have manifested—your specific behavior. You may be unsure about how much you should reveal. What level of detail is appropriate? This is something you will need to negotiate with your partner.

The guideline we generally give is that you need to disclose all the significant ways you have acted out, but you don't necessarily need to provide every specific sexual detail. However, if there are other people involved, you will need to let her know who those people are. If they are people she knows or may meet, she needs to know their names. If there is any kind of possible exposure to disease or infection involved, you will need to provide those details.

For example, if your issue is masturbating to porn on the Internet, you will need to tell her the type of porn websites you go to, how often you have tended to go there, and any repercussions you may have suffered because you have been engaged in your compulsion—such as getting in trouble at work. If you have been going online to chat rooms, tell her about the type of chat rooms you have visited and the type of conversations you had there. If you have been flirting with your coworkers, friends, or strangers, you need to let her know the nature of the flirting.

If you have had sex (unprotected or not) with others, you need to let her know the specific nature and level of physical contact. If you have had any kind of sex with another, it is important that she get a checkup with her doctor, even if you are certain that you could not have passed on any kind of disease or infection. This precaution is important so both of you can have peace of mind and a fresh start.

Be sure to tell her each element of your acting out. Again, you don't need to provide every sexual detail, but you do need to be sure you have told her about every significant type of behavior. In order to rebuild trust, she will need to know that you haven't left anything out. You don't want her to discover something significant later by getting a phone call, talking to a friend, or hearing about a sexually transmitted disease from her doctor.

Let your partner guide you about the amount of detail she would like to have concerning types of behaviors, names of people, number of encounters, dates, places, expense, or any other specifics she would like to know. Each person will have their own level of comfort with the level of detail they need to hear. Keep in mind that comparing your partner to someone else is not necessary and will probably only be hurtful.

Each person has their own needs in terms of level of detail that they would like to hear. For some people, more details are reassuring; for others, specifics are hurtful. To understand this, think of the description you would give to a friend if you got a bad cut on your finger that required stitches. Some people might want to hear every detail about how you got the cut and might even want to see the stitches. Someone else might be satisfied with simply knowing that you cut your finger. That person may not even want to see the bandage.

If you are reading this book, we're assuming that your partner already knows at least some of what you have done. A big part of your reluctance to tell is simply that you feel guilty. No one wants to mess up. However, if you do not reveal what you have been trying to hide, the secret will impact you and your relationship negatively in a number of ways. Your partner's imagination about what you have done is generally more destructive to your relationship than the truth about your compulsive, addictive sexual behavior.

Too many times, we have seen the person who has been sexually compulsive make the mistake of not telling his partner everything she wants to know. Because part of the problem is that he has been holding back, if he continues to do so, the problem will not be resolved.

The more honest you are now, the better the chance of saving the relationship. This level of disclosure will probably be uncomfortable because you are likely to feel ashamed, embarrassed, or guilty. You may feel like the kid who has been caught with his hand in the cookie jar. But don't be like the kid who denies that he has taken the cookies. Go ahead and admit to everything you have done. In the long run, this will be in your best interest and in the best interest of your relationship.

Finally, you need to apologize, without excuses. Say, "I'm sorry I've hurt you in this way," "I'm sorry I've lied to you," "I'm sorry I've put you at risk." This would not be the time to bring up any issues or unhappiness you feel about your partner. There is no legitimate excuse for acting out sexually. Simply say, "I'm sorry" and let her know specifically what you are sorry for doing. This is important. In our experience, most men are desperate to give reasons and excuses for their behavior. Those impulses are normal, but don't follow them. This is simply the moment to reveal and apologize.

For Her: He Has Something to Tell You

When your partner tells you the details of how he has betrayed the intimacy of his connection with you, you will likely feel some apprehension and some relief. The most important thing to remember is that his acting out has nothing to do with you. It has nothing to do with your sexuality or desirability, or your value as a human. This is his inappropriate way of dealing with issues and feelings that he has not previously known how to endure.

This is also the time for you to tell all. If you have any suspicions that have not been voiced, state them. Ask for any details you want to hear. There may be some specifics you would just as soon not know. You may or may not want to hear specific sexual details like the types of porn sites your partner has visited, the names or types of people with whom he has engaged sexually, or the elements of a sexual encounter. Maybe you are not ready to hear this sort of detail, and maybe you will be ready next week, next year, or never. Take care of yourself and respect your feelings. Part of respecting your feelings is sharing them with your partner. If you have felt hurt, betrayed, angry, sad, or disappointed, be honest and clear.

Share your feelings without blaming. Although your feelings are in response to his behavior, they are still your feelings. He may have done things that have caused these feelings to arise, but they are your feelings. If you have feelings of being hurt, sad, angry—whatever you may feel—that is perfectly normal.

Right now, you don't need to forgive or feel compassion for your partner. That may come in time, but it is not necessary right now. Your feelings of understanding, forgiveness, and compassion will probably ebb and flow for a while. It is important to let him say everything he has to say without stopping him before you comment. When he is finished, let him know exactly how you feel. Tell him as specifically as you can without attacking him personally.

By this, we mean you may want to tell him how hurt you are, how angry you are, or how numb you feel. You can express all that without telling him what a rotten person he is or how he is exactly like his father or your father or some despicable character you know. After he has shared with you, you will quite possibly need time to be alone and reflect on what you have heard.

For Him: How to Bear Her Reaction

Now that you have finally "come clean" and revealed all the worst of you, you probably feel that you deserve a big pat on the back for your courage and honesty. And you do deserve kudos—this is a big and important step. But your partner may be sad, angry, distant, or some combination of those emotions. It is normal for you to feel good about what you have accomplished so far. And it is normal that your partner is still processing what she has heard from you. At this time, it is important that you simply acknowledge your partner's feelings. Skillful responses include, "I understand" and "I'm sorry."

It is perfectly normal if you have the impulse to defend yourself by explaining your actions or blaming your partner. But don't do it! This impulse is part of your survival mechanism. You want to protect yourself by fending off what feels like an attack. Or you may have an urge to just run away. When you can recognize this impulse for what it is, you will recognize that you have the option to make a different choice about your response.

As much as you can, put yourself in your partner's shoes and compassionately hear her response, and you will be able to lay the groundwork for the rebuilding of her trust.

Many men have reported that because their partner's response is difficult to bear, they have intense urges to engage in their familiar sexually compulsive behaviors. It can be helpful to find ways to get the support that your partner might not be able to provide. You may need someone to help you with your urges to fight back, run away, or act out. And you may want to receive recognition for your efforts. This would be the time to speak with a good friend, counselor, support group, trusted family member, or your pastor.

CHAPTER SUMMARY

- **Reassurances for her:**

  1. You are not responsible for your partner's sexually addictive behaviors. His choices about how he deals with his irritations and stimulations are his alone, as are yours.
  2. Your partner's sexually addictive actions are not an indication that he does not love you. Your relationship is not hopeless or doomed because your partner has a problem with sexual compulsivity.
  3. You are not weak or damaged because you want to stay with your partner and rebuild your relationship.

4. You don't have to force yourself to trust your partner right now. It is normal to feel angry, upset, and mistrusting.
5. You don't need to go through this time alone. Reach out to friends, family, and other support systems.

- **Reassurances for him:**

1. Being a sex addict does not mean you are a failure.
2. You can stop acting out sexually. Once you do that, your relationship has a chance to survive, change, and become more intimate and fulfilling.
3. Having an issue with sexual compulsivity does not mean you do not love your partner. It does mean you have an issue with intimacy.
4. You may not know how to stop your sexually addictive behaviors, but you can commit to finding a way to stop them and to building intimacy with your partner.
5. You don't need to go through this time alone. Reach out to friends, family, and other support systems.

Looking Forward

In Chapter 5, which opens Part 2, we begin by looking at re-establishing trust as a first step. Other chapters in Part 2 explore areas that are typically roadblocks to healing and creating deeper intimacy, understanding the toxic cycle of shame and blame, and working with strong feelings and emotions. Learning to work with strong emotions not only helps you develop deeper intimacy, it also helps you develop the necessary capacity to work with addictive urges.

PART TWO

REBUILDING YOUR RELATIONSHIP

CHAPTER 5

Re-Establishing Trust on the Road to Forgiveness

You've survived the initial storm. You've lived through the shock of revelation. Internet porn, pornographic videos, prostitutes, sexually intriguing chatting online or in e-mails, or sexually explicit text messages have intruded upon your intimate sexual relationship, or an affair or a series of affairs has been revealed. The problem is no longer hidden. Both partners have probably experienced moments of surprising relief from starkly viewing the truth of the problem. The secret is finally out.

Just as in any disaster, after the destruction, there comes a time when you have assessed the nature of the damage and may have determined you will attempt to rebuild. But how do you begin? This is an important moment. It's valuable to pause and acknowledge the strength of character required to get this far.

If you are the one who has been betrayed, you have borne humiliation and the shattering of illusion. You have discovered that what you thought existed actually does not exist. The love and/or the relationship that you thought you had is not what you believed it was. It may be helpful to know that many couples have been able to find their way through the shock of the revelation and have been able to rebuild trust and strengthen their relationships.

What's Left?

Initially, you may not be able to see or articulate exactly why, but you have enough certainty in your connection with your partner that you have chosen to begin the process of rebuilding. You recognize that the connection you have can be painful and challenging, but you have a desire or internal imperative to find a way to repair and rebuild what has been broken.

What Is Trust?

Wanting to trust and wanting to be trusted is a natural part of being human. At a core level, each of us just wants to love and be loved; trust is part of that process. The state of being able to trust (or not) is developed early in our relationships with the adults who were caring for us—generally our mothers and fathers, usually primarily our mothers. At a young age, as we begin to differentiate and move away from the safety of our parents' direct sphere and then safely return, we begin to build internal trust structures. We begin to determine that we can trust ourselves in the world.

These trusting structures are internally strengthened in those moments when we as children have a frightening or maddening (or otherwise uncomfortable) experience and are able to bring that experience back to the safety of our adult caregiver and be comforted, validated, and accepted. In the moment of experiencing the uncomfortable impulse, we see that we are still safe. We understand that we are uncomfortable, but we are still okay. We start to build the internal structure that can contain the discomfort.

To the extent that we were not able to build trust structures in our formative years, our intimate relationships become the place where we have the greatest difficulties with trust. Often, we project our fear or lack of trust onto our partner. Both partners often share this lack of capacity to trust.

Joe and Maggie

Joe lives in the heartland of the country with his wife Maggie and their three kids. He has been masturbating to porn since he was twelve. It started with the Sears catalog, and then he found his father's stash of *Playboy* magazines. His parents were both alcoholics. He learned early on that he couldn't trust them; he never knew what he would find when he came home from school. He did not get trust structures in place when he was growing up.

Consequently, as his sexuality was budding, he didn't trust that he could count on a live woman to be there for him, but he could count on images. And now, the women he can rely on to be there for him are those constantly available images on his computer screen. All he has to do is turn on his computer.

Ironically, Joe's wife would actually like to have sex with him, but it is difficult for him to ask for sex. He does not trust that if she says no he will have the strength to bear that momentary rejection. He gave up on that kind of trust so long ago.

This lack of trust is not something that was immediately apparent to Joe. As he began to look at where he had trust and where he did not, he began to see how difficult it was for him to trust, or to allow the feeling of safety with another.

Trusting Yourself

We all understand that after trust has been broken in a relationship, it naturally needs to be rebuilt. Paradoxically, trust not only needs to be restored in the relationship between the two partners, it also needs to be repaired internally by each partner. If you are the one who has been acting in an untrustworthy way, it will be difficult for you to believe that you can trust yourself. And because you don't trust yourself, it will be difficult for you to trust anyone else. It is very common for the partner who has been acting out sexually to discover how he does not trust his mate.

Lack of internal trust is a fundamental cornerstone of addictive behavior—it keeps you in the grip of your coping strategy. It allows the shame part of the addictive cycle to grab you. Finding ways to put your sexually compulsive behavior on hold is not only step one in rebuilding trust with your partner, it is also step one in rebuilding trust in yourself. And rebuilding trust in yourself helps you control your compulsive impulses. In learning how to tolerate your negative feelings, you build the internal structure that allows you to see that you may feel extremely uncomfortable in a given moment, but you are still okay. When you begin to know that you can survive the painful impulses you are having, then the grip that the sexually addictive coping strategy has on you is loosened.

Broken Trust

One of the spokes on the wheel of sexual addiction is shame. Shame leads to the desire to cover up, and covering up leads to lying—outright false statements, and lies of omission. Such lies are one of the most troubling parts of the addictive behavior for the partner of an addict.

If you are sexually compulsive, you may recognize by now that the sexually addictive behaviors that objectify women—behaviors such as using porn excessively, flirting inappropriately, going to adult entertainment locations or websites, engaging in affairs—are hurtful to your partner. They prevent you from engaging intimately. These behaviors quite obviously break the bonds of intimacy. They damage the relationship and impair trust. But we often hear from partners that the factor that is the hardest to reconcile, the hardest to forgive, is the lying.

Let's put this in perspective. As human animals, a part of how we naturally navigate in our world is through what we experience as normalcy, as regularity. We get out of bed in the morning and know that the sky will be up, the ground will be down, our eyes will be our eye color, our hair (if we have any) will be our hair color. When shocking events occur that are out of our expectations, we become destabilized. Our brains need time to reorder and reintegrate the new information.

If a man is having an affair, is cruising for prostitutes, or is spending late hours at work masturbating to porn, some people believe that his partner somehow intuitively knows. We have not experienced that to be true. Quite often, the partner of a sex addict does not know anything about the nature of her partner's activities. However, she generally does suspect that something is off. Generally, she has questioned her partner about a suspicion and he has lied in response to her query. She senses something to be true ("things are not quite right") and the person she trusts, her intimate partner, is telling her that her senses are wrong ("things are fine") when really she is not wrong. This is destabilizing. She begins to question her perception of reality. When she finally does begin to see the truth of her suspicions, not only has her ability to trust her partner been damaged, her capacity to trust her own sense of reality has been impaired.

Often, someone in the grip of addiction can, in a given moment, so fervently believe his own lies that the deceitful fabrication can actually register as truth to his partner. It is important for both partners to understand and hold compassion for the destabilizing that has occurred because of the lies. The bottom line here is that if you have been lying to your partner, you have rocked her sense of reality. If your partner has been lying to you, your sense of reality has been distorted. Distorted reality can make you feel kind of crazy. Recovering from that takes time. It begins with simply admitting to what has been done and hearing the admission. The admission then needs to be followed by telling the truth again and again and again—in what we call an "undefended" way. In Chapter 8, we discuss more fully the process of undefended honesty.

Megan and Steve

Megan and Steve met in their mid-forties, and both felt they had finally found the person who really understood them. In the beginning of their marriage, they felt deep love, connection, and passion for each other. They both reported that early in their marriage their sex life was passionate and satisfying.

Steve had inherited his family's property, so Megan and Steve lived in Steve's childhood home. After they had been married for about four years and Steve bought a new computer, Megan began to notice that they were having sex less and less often, and that Steve was spending a lot of time with his new computer. He was staying up late to play video games for four to five hours most nights. But Steve didn't want to talk about the video games. To Megan this was uncharacteristic and suspicious. Megan decided to check the computer to find out what was so engaging to her husband. You have probably guessed the rest of the story.

Steve was visiting porn websites—websites with content that was shocking to Megan. She hadn't even imagined that portrayals of sex with such young girls existed. So she decided to see if she could find more evidence about what Steve had been doing. She looked in the closets of Steve's family house that had not been cleaned out for over twenty years, and discovered boxes and boxes of porn videos and magazines.

Initially, when she confronted Steve with her discoveries, he denied that the videos were his or that he had visited the porn websites. In fact, he yelled at Megan for intruding on his privacy. Megan wasn't certain what to do about what she had found, but she was clear that she couldn't live with this behavior. She told Steve she was moving out in one week unless he could at least admit what he had been doing. During that week, Megan felt the pain of the possibility that her relationship with Steve might indeed be over. She slept in their spare bedroom and ate her meals alone.

It took Steve that full week, but he eventually admitted what he had been doing. He was not yet ready to acknowledge the content of the sexually explicit material he had been accessing on the Internet to stimulate himself. And he wasn't ready to talk about the porn videos and porn magazines that had been accumulating since the time he was in high school.

Megan was initially relieved to hear just this portion of the truth. She was certain that there was more to the story, and she didn't know how she could trust Steve until he told her everything. She also felt betrayed that he had lied to her about the video tapes and that he was attracted to websites that were so abhorrent to her. She couldn't imagine how she could again engage with him in a sexual way while knowing that he was captivated by the images she had seen on the computer screen.

Megan wanted to be able to trust Steve and Steve wanted Megan to trust him. Steve felt frozen, guilty, and embarrassed. Neither one of them could imagine how they could regain the love and connection they had initially experienced with each other. They hoped there was a way to come back together, but could not imagine how to navigate from Point A to Point B.

How to Begin to Rebuild Trust

When a couple is wrestling with the issue of sex addiction, the man has usually been acting out sexually and the woman is hurt and loses trust in the relationship. At the end of Chapter 4, we provided an exercise for making full disclosure of the sexually compulsive behavior. If you haven't completed that step, it won't be possible to begin the task of rebuilding trust. When there is an elephant in the living room, it will be necessary to know how the elephant got into the living room. But when you have an elephant in the living room, it's important to first get it out. That elephant is causing a lot of destruction. Most importantly, it's impossible to rebuild trust while the elephant is still in the living room!

It's probably obvious to you that it's impossible for a couple to have a conversation about couple dynamics or about how to rebuild trust while one partner is acting violently or drinking alcohol to excess or abusing drugs. In the same way, the sexually acting-out behaviors must at least be put on pause. Even if the stopping is not perfect, there must be the desire to stop and there must be some kind of structure put in place to support the stopping.

Just hoping or imagining that you will be able to stop compulsive behavior is wishful thinking. When the noise caused by the destructive behavior is quieted, then the issues that may be triggering the destructive acting out can be addressed. Building the capacity and skill to address the underlying issues are precisely the ingredients that lead to the rebuilding of trust and compassion.

Any relationship is a dance, and if one partner changes his or her dance steps it will necessarily impact the other partner for the good or the bad. Since none of us is perfect, in every troubled relationship both members of the couple are contributing in some fashion to the disharmony. However, when one partner's behavior is destructive, "big" in a way that overshadows other aspects of the relationship, and compulsive, it tends to take up all the air space. The focus is on the sexually addicted partner and on his or her compulsive behavior.

If you are the partner who has been acting out, undoubtedly you have some issues with your partner that you'd like for her to hear. Just know that in order for your issues to be heard, you must first stop your sexually addictive behavior. When you do, your chances of finding the compassion, understanding, and trust that you want from your partner are much greater. If the destructive behavior continues, the relationship should not continue. Even if your partner manages to stick with you, resentment, anger, and distrust will prevent the understanding and forgiveness you desire from blooming.

Often, the partner in a couple who is acting out sexually feels that he has been labeled as the bad one, the one who is causing all the trouble, the identified patient or IP. We've often heard the complaint in our offices from husbands who are feeling blamed, "I'm not the IP here." In Chapter 6, we will focus more specifically on how you can work with blame and shame. In the meantime, if you are the partner who has been acting out sexually, realize that you are likely to remain the focus of the issues in the relationship until you can get control over your compensatory acting-out behaviors. Once you get the elephant out of the living room, you can begin to learn how to keep it out of the living room, and how it got into the living room in the first place. You will be able to investigate the nature of the elephant. And most importantly, you can start to restore the living room.

Acting out sexually (or any compensatory addictive behavior) is a distraction from being able to see the underlying issue. Addictive behavior is an avoidance of something. It is about wanting comfort. The addictive behavior is a compulsion that is triggered because you don't want to feel what you are feeling. It has the added component of the wired-in biological rush that is experienced in the moment of orgasm. In Chapters 6 and 7, we will address building the skill of experiencing what you don't want to feel. Building this capacity will be a tremendous support in dealing with compulsive urges. Additionally, for both of you, building the skills of dealing with shame and blame and of working with strong feelings and emotions create the pathway to building greater intimacy for you as a couple.

The Outcome of Being Trustworthy

We often disappoint each other and ourselves, in large and small ways. You may have the notion that rebuilding trust means living happily ever after. When we first begin a relationship, we are in the flush of possibility. We are often at the height of sexual connection and attraction. There is a natural and innocent sense of love, connection, and trust. When the relationship is shattered by lies and betrayal, you may wish you could reset the relationship back to the beginning. That won't happen.

But there is a beauty in the tempering that occurs in walking through the crisis. Some relationships will survive and others will not. Rebuilding trust takes time and attention.

As mentioned, the most important trust to foster is the trust in yourself. The trust between the two partners rests upon that structure. Even though your relationship as you knew it is irrevocably shattered, what can arise from the ashes can be deeper and more solid than before. Forgiveness is a byproduct of the rebuilding of trust. And trust is built by 1) telling the truth, 2) by being able to live with your discomfort about that truth, and 3) by being able to live with your partner's reactions to that truth.

As one wife wrote to her husband:

I have come to realize that trusting you does not mean that in any individual circumstance you will give me what I think I want. It does not mean that in the future I will not be hurt by something you say or do or do not say or do. It does not mean that you will not disappoint me. But because you have been so willing to tell me the entire truth about what you have done, I am coming to see that you have the strength of character to bear my reaction and that feels trustworthy to me.

The Broken Teacup

There's an old story about a broken teacup that we would like to tell in our own way to illustrate this portion of your journey. It is a story about a beautiful bone china teacup that has been passed down from generation to generation. This teacup is displayed carefully on a special shelf above the fireplace. One day when the wife is carefully placing the teacup on the shelf, it drops on the floor and shatters.

Heartsick, the wife gathers the pieces together and carefully, over many weeks, reassembles the teacup, gluing it together piece after piece. When she is finished, she is still heartbroken because the beautiful pristine china is no longer as it was. It has been put back together, but to her it appears to be a monstrosity.

As in many good stories, a wise old woman comes to visit, and the wife cries, telling the old woman she no longer has a beautiful teacup in which to serve tea to her guests. The wise old woman points out the beauty of the mended teacup. The teacup is now stronger in each place the glue has bonded piece to piece and the lines of the bonding form a beautiful and elegant pattern showing the immense care with which the teacup has been reassembled. She points out that it is not the same teacup as it was originally, but it is now a stronger cup reflective of the love and care that has been put into it.

Exercise: Experiencing Trust

This exercise can be done in your home, but is best done in some unfamiliar but safe place. Partners stand side to side, both facing the same direction, arms touching. One partner will be the guide and the other the follower; then the roles will be reversed.

Decide who will be the first guide. The follower closes his or her eyes and keeps them closed. The guide puts one arm around the follower's waist, and with the other holds the follower's arm or hand.

Begin to walk. The guide, keeping eyes open, guides the follower as they walk so they don't walk into something or fall. Working together, both partners navigate through space as cooperatively as possible for 3–5 minutes. Then switch roles.

After the exercise: Answer these questions individually and then share your answers with your partner.

- When you were guiding your partner, what was your experience of being responsible for your partner?
- When your eyes were closed and you were being guided by your partner, what was your experience of needing to trust your partner?

This exercise helps you directly experience your relationship around trust with another. There is no correct or incorrect experience. Whatever you experience is information to help you better understand your relationship to trust and feeling safe. Individuals have reported feeling apprehensive with their eyes closed; others have reported feeling safe and relaxed. The partner guiding may feel scared with the responsibility or may feel exhilarated about being in charge. Let yourself be surprised and informed.

For example, one man who believed he was a "tough guy" had a revealing experience doing this exercise. He reported that while being guided by his partner, he shuffled and had a hard time walking. It was difficult to let go, to trust. When the roles were reversed and he was guiding his partner, he was aware that he felt like he was "holding a butterfly." He became aware of the tenderness that he actually feels and wants to experience in dealing not only with his partner but also with the world. He reported that it felt good to take care of his wife in this simple way. He had cared for his family financially, had given his wife flowers and jewelry, but had not previously recognized how wonderful and precious it was to have the responsibility of tenderly holding someone's welfare in his hands, to be trustworthy.

CHAPTER SUMMARY

- Many couples have been able to find their way through the shock of the revelation of sexually addictive behaviors and have been able not only to rebuild trust but to actually strengthen their relationship.
- We each want to love and be loved. Trusting and being trusted is a part of the equation of love.
- The state of being able to trust (or not) is developed early in our relationships with the adults who were caring for us.
- Trust not only needs to be restored in the relationship between the two partners, it also needs to be repaired internally by each partner. Lack of internal trust is a fundamental cornerstone of addictive behavior.

- Rebuilding trust takes time and attention. The most important trust to foster is the trust in yourself. The trust between the two partners rests upon that structure.
- Trust is built by 1) telling the truth, 2) by being able to live with your discomfort about that truth, and 3) by being able to live with your partner's reactions to that truth.

Looking Forward

Many behaviors can stand in the way of trust. Chapter 6 uncovers how to work with yourself and with your partner in dealing with the inevitable cycle of shame and blame.

CHAPTER 6

Working with Shame and Blame

By now, you have begun to understand some of the impulses and patterns of sex addiction in your relationship. You have found your way through the first days or weeks of the discovery or revelation that sexual compulsivity is a problem in your relationship. Often, you will encounter a cycle of blame and shame that can feel like a maze with no escape.

The partner who has acted out sexually is deeply familiar with shame. As with any addiction, the compulsive partner is ashamed that he (or she) can't control the behavior. The shame creates discomfort that causes the compulsive partner to act out sexually, so the cycle repeats. Additionally, even though the sexually compulsive individual may not be openly voicing this to his partner, he often has an internal blame dialog going on about how he did not get and/or is not getting what he wants and needs. (And, in many cases, it is probably true that he is not getting what he wants and feels he needs.) It is not surprising that there is an impulse to do something to try to get rid of the shame. Shame feels terrible. Blame can be a familiar and handy tool.

The partner who has been betrayed also usually feels shame in many ways, such as shame about being rejected by her partner. After all, he has chosen to be with other people sexually (whether images or actual people) rather than being with her. She often feels shame about being perceived as someone who would be in and remain in such a relationship. She probably also feels shame for her partner. She often has concerns about talking about what is going on with her partner because she doesn't want her partner to look bad in the eyes of her friends and family. She blames her partner for engaging in actions that have created difficulty for the couple. She is not getting what she wants and feels she needs.

Although it is natural to focus on the behaviors of the partner who has been acting out sexually, particularly initially, it has been shown that true healing occurs by focusing on the couple's dynamic, not just on the partner who is sexually compulsive. In particular, we have found that the dynamics of blame and shame tend to be highly activated for both partners, especially during the times of discovery, disclosure, or the unraveling of one partner's acting out in a compulsive way.

The pattern of shame and blame grabs each partner in its own special and probably familiar way. Also, in shame and blame there tends to be a game of musical chairs. The partner relegated to "loser"—the partner who doesn't get to sit in the chair when the music stops—can flip between each of the pair. Each partner tends to want the other person to be the source of the problem. In truth, in the game of blame and shame, both partners are losers. There is no chair to sit in when the music stops. There is no winner when we are trapped by our shame mechanisms.

The storyline of blame and shame tends to be different for each of the partners, but the underlying structures are generally remarkably similar for both. We tend to mirror each other in surprising ways. Let's begin the investigation of how shame and blame work so that as a couple you can learn how to both be winners when shame comes to visit.

The Seeds of Shame

As mentioned in Chapter 1, we quite naturally require human connection at a biological level. We have evolved as members of a tribe and as part of a society. We need each other. Our connection with one another brings meaning, purpose, and joy into our lives.

However, in order to live in groups, we need to learn what is acceptable and what is unacceptable; otherwise, our society doesn't work. We would live in chaos. We need to internally gain the structures of being able to discern right from wrong, good from bad, so we can comfortably live as part of the group. Instinctively, we know that being kicked out of our group would be dangerous to our survival. We want to belong, and we need to belong.

Our training in becoming productive humans requires discipline. We need to learn not to hit our friend because he made us angry, not to scream and throw a temper tantrum because we can't have ice cream, or not to run out into the street. We need to learn, "No, don't do that, that behavior is unacceptable."

Shame arises when we mistakenly associate unacceptable or "bad" with who we are inherently rather than simply with our actions. When we associate bad with our actions (not with our being), then we can appropriately recognize that our actions require some modification. We can appropriately feel guilt and remorse, which are part of a healthy correcting mechanism. We recognize that our action was in error, and then choose to take a different course of action in the future.

We naturally learn by trial and error. We can even make a huge error and experience huge guilt and remorse, but still recognize that it was an error of action and not a fundamental flaw in the core essence of who we are.

While it doesn't necessarily feel good to experience guilt and remorse, it does not touch the heart of who we are—our core "me-ness," our wholeness. We can deeply regret a mistaken action or choice, but our self-love, our self-acceptance has not been impacted. Recognizing we made a mistake is far different than believing we are a mistake.

Believing we are a mistake is the fuel of shame. The shame voice inside of you says, *I am inherently bad, or worthless, or unredeemable, or evil, or defective, or useless, or broken,* or whatever words you internally apply to yourself. This voice may speak to you at times in a whisper, at times in a scream. You may not hear the voice of your shame directly; you may just feel it as a sense of dread or foreboding.

Brené Brown, a research professor at the University of Houston Graduate College of Social Work, an expert on shame and its impact, speaks of a shame epidemic. Her research has led her to conclude that the perfectionistic drives of our society have taken us on a wild goose chase to achieve the unachievable, to become extraordinary. She has concluded that shame is not an effective motivating influence; it is more likely to cause destructive behaviors than to cure them. Shame is correlated with the compensatory behaviors we use to attempt to get away from bad feelings—reactions such as the numbing-out strategies of addictive behaviors or those of aggression and violent action.

This means that internally we have a broken motivational system. The system of guilt (I *did* something bad) leads to remorse. That allows us to make a different choice. Unfortunately, this kind of functional motivational system is being co-opted by the internally destructive mechanism of shame (I *am* bad).

More Shame and Blame Is Not the Answer

Your broken system of shame is not a cause for more shame or blame. Your parents, teachers, and other authorities—the people who trained you—probably spoke to you in ways that were shaming, and now you have incorporated those shaming voices into your internal structures. You are the product of your heritage, as your parents, teachers, and other authority figures were the products of their heritage. You now have the opportunity to respond differently for yourself and for everyone you contact.

It's not necessarily simple to alter this internal pattern. Using your shame system to get yourself to change won't eradicate your shame system. Changing any deeply engrained system takes time and attention, but the alternative is continuing to be at the mercy of the impact of the mechanisms of shame. We believe it is skillful (and compassionate) to assume that you will need to work with your internal shame mechanisms in some fashion, to some degree, for the rest of your life. However, it is certainly possible to gain skill and expertise in doing so and thus increase your capacity for vulnerability, compassion, and intimacy.

The Antidote to Shame

First, you just need to notice how you are using shame as an internal regulator. Watch how shame works inside of you. Do you lash out, run away, freeze up, become seductive—all of the above? Do you hear shame, see it internally, feel it, sense it—all of the above? How do you align internally with your shame mechanism? How do you fight against it? Neither the aligning nor the fighting against it is going to be effective; you can't fight against it. Why? Because you will just be fighting against yourself. The structure is a part of you. You have internalized the shaming voices of your domestication.

The antidote is compassion for yourself first. The word "compassion" comes from Latin, and literally means "to suffer with." Just like a crying baby is not comforted by hatred but by tenderness, your internalized "badness" is not comforted by attempting to expel it but by accepting, by making friends with the uncomfortable feeling you are having. Compassion is a quality that arises in a moment of allowing yourself to be undefended, to be vulnerable.

We recognize that it feels counterintuitive to move toward vulnerability when you are experiencing shame. Shame feels bad, and we all quite naturally want to get away from it, eradicate it, kill it, at least blame someone else for it! In Chapter 7, we will speak more fully about the mechanism of letting go of your uncomfortably strong feelings and emotions and developing vulnerability.

Shame: It Just Won't Listen to Reason

Attempting to reason with your shame, using logic or positive self-talk, can be just another form of engaging in a battle with your feelings of shame. Letting go into vulnerability is often experienced as a leap of faith. It can feel as if you are standing on the edge of a cliff and all of your instinctive protection is telling you to get out of there—to fight, to flee, to freeze. Vulnerability is required to leap into compassion. Reasoning can get you to the edge of the cliff. You can read these words, understand them, understand the mechanism, but the letting go requires a giving up of control. Just for a moment, when you recognize that your protective impulses are telling you that you are in danger but you aren't really in danger, in that instant, even as a momentary experiment, stop protecting. Let the experience of shame have you, become vulnerable to it. You do not have to maintain the facade of perfection.

You can tell yourself, "I am not really bad" when you are feeling shame, but we're guessing you have tried that over and over. Someone else can tell you, "You are not really bad," and we bet you've tried that one, too. That is the approach of reasoning, of arguing. It can provide temporary solace, and can be helpful, but right now we are looking at how you can get to the root of the shame mechanism.

The Limits of Reason and Logic

If you are looking for a good restaurant, you may peruse a number of different restaurant menus. Then when you choose the place you want, you go to the restaurant, order your meal, and when it comes you enjoy it (hopefully!). Reviewing all of those menus helped you choose a restaurant. Studying the menu of the restaurant you chose helped you decide what to order. They were great tools to assist you in getting to the point of actually receiving the food. But eating even one of those restaurant menus itself would not be satisfying or helpful. In the same way, using reason and logic can help you understand shame mechanism, but won't, on its own, get rid of the shame. It is helpful and necessary to learn how you conclude that you are unworthy of acceptance and belonging. This understanding allows you to recognize that your shame mechanism has been activated. It is helpful to use your intellect to build your self-esteem. But the gnawing sense of shame, that you are inherently flawed, is not relieved by greater self-esteem, words, or even understanding the concept that you are not bad.

The Leather Earth

The outcome of greater vulnerability is the building of greater compassion internally, and greater compassion internally leads to greater compassion for others. This compassion and vulnerability fosters greater intimacy. But there is a pitfall that many of us make on our road to seeking greater intimacy.

We have heard a story about Jeradiah, who long, long ago lamented the pain of walking the earth in his bare feet. He was tired of the cuts, bruises, and blisters that came from treading over rocks, hot sand, and thorny plants. So he went to his friend Horatio to get some help. His idea was that if he and Horatio could simply cover the earth in the skins of animals, cover the entire ground in leather, then he and everyone else could be free of the torment of their journeying. Horatio, being an extremely wise soul, carefully considered Jeradiah's proposal and then offered an alternative suggestion. "Jeradiah," he said, "what if, instead of the monumental and I'm afraid impossible task of covering the entire earth in leather, you were to simply cover your feet in leather!"

The experience of shame is relieved by compassion for yourself. This compassion is reached through vulnerability—by allowing yourself to be undefended. In the moment of recognizing that you are in the midst of a shame storm, you have the opportunity to choose vulnerability rather than fighting, fleeing, or freezing. The menu is not the meal; the map is not the journey. The tools and your understandings have gotten you to this point. The liberation from shame is in letting go internally to the vulnerability of compassion rather than hatred.

It is so easy to make the mistake (particularly with your intimate partner) of assuming that if you can get him or her to just stop doing those annoying things then you will not have to feel the discomfort of shame. You can so easily fall into the trap of, "I want you to do or not do ____________________, so that I will feel or not feel ____________________." You can attempt to cover your entire earth in leather. But it's just not possible. However, you can skillfully cover your feet in leather by recognizing and applying compassion to your own internal mechanism of shame. You can begin to recognize how you are gripped by "I am bad.'"

The capacity to feed yourself with compassion frees both you and your partner from having to behave in a particular way to prevent shame from coming to visit.

Pointing Fingers: The Tricks of Blame

This understanding does not mean that you have license to do or say whatever you want, and then if your partner has a bad reaction, you can just tell your partner to "do their work" or to "get over it." That thinking is actually the opposite of the responsibility for oneself that we are describing. If you are in the midst of a disagreement with your partner, attempting to tell your partner about his or her faulty thinking is only a trick of blame. If you stick with righteous indignation, you avoid feeling the pain of what is arising. Then you will not be able to take responsibility for your part.

If you catch yourself in the "who started it" game, you have distracted yourself from the real investigation. Although we've all probably done it, this kind of finger-pointing technique is just another form of playing musical chairs with no chair for a winner—everyone loses. If you or your partner catch yourselves in the "who started it" or "who is at fault" game, then you have a clue that you are probably caught in a cycle of shame and blame. When you experience shame, you may find yourself trying to get the shame away from you by making it the other's fault. More than likely, your partner has indeed done something that has caused your internal shame mechanism to flare.

Another Visit to Jeannine and Jay

Jeannine and Jay (whom you met at the beginning of Chapter 1) could not seem to unravel their major fights over what seemed to be, even to them, minor matters. You may recall that they noticed they were irritated with each other much of the time. Jay was finally able to admit to Jeannine that he had been masturbating while looking at porn almost every night at his office. He and Jeannine both felt relief that what had previously been a secret was now out in the open.

However, Jeannine and Jay also recognized that they needed to find out what was causing their ongoing irritation with each other and how that might be playing into Jay's attempts to escape into the world of porn. They both understood how important it was to uncover their own motivations in this story that was heading for a very unhappy ending. They saw that in order to address the sexual compulsivity issues inside their relationship, they needed to understand their blame and shame dynamics. Jay had agreed to stop looking at the porn, but he was very aware that his desire to stop was not enough. They both knew they needed to find a way to address the lack of closeness that was manifesting as bickering over what seemed to be minor matters.

They were able to identify that the fight that really seemed to have a life of its own was an ongoing disagreement about the kitchen sink sponge. Jeannine would become irritated that Jay would not remember to squeeze out the sponge when he used it and place it on the edge of the sink. For Jay, it didn't make any sense that he could not simply leave the sponge in the bottom of the sink where it would be ready for use the next time. Even when he did try to remember to squeeze out the sponge, he didn't seem to be able to squeeze it in a way that was satisfactory to Jeannine. He felt Jeannine was being overly critical and uptight about a matter that he viewed as trivial. He felt that she was just picking on him.

Each one of them blamed the other for the problem, but ultimately, they were able to find the underlying motivations that were contributing to this particular disagreement and humorously label this ongoing fight "the saga of the sponge." How did they get there?

Let's start by looking at this through Jay's eyes. First, he was able to recognize what he was feeling when it seemed that Jeannine was "going after him" about the sponge. He was able to see that he was instantly being transported into the land of imperfection, which he connected with being flawed, or inherently bad. He saw how much he really wanted to please Jeannine so he could maintain his sense of perfection and then not have to experience his wounded inherent feeling of badness. He saw how he felt he could not tolerate making a mistake in Jeannine's eyes because if he did make a mistake, he instantly experienced not being extraordinary, not being perfect—that he was inherently bad.

This experience of imperfection happened instantly, faster than his thinking mind could register. So, he instinctively and reflexively pushed his feeling of being bad (shame) away. He wanted to make this bad feeling Jeannine's fault: "If she would just stop nagging me about the sponge, then I wouldn't feel angry. Everything would be fine." He began to be able to recognize that when he felt this being bad/shame reaction, he instantly felt angry and wanted to yell at Jeannine. Then he began to be able to see that all the yelling in the world was not going to heal his internal sense of being bad. This is where his internal compassion began to come into play.

He began to be able to recognize that the urge to yell at Jeannine could be a signal that what he really wanted (and needed) was to finally give some comfort to his sense of inherent badness. He was able to see how he had internalized the messages from his childhood about how stupid, selfish, and overly sensitive he was. He began to be able to see that his internal sense of being bad, his shame, had been put into place long ago. Jeannine was unwittingly creating a shame storm in Jay when she had her own impulsive negative reaction whenever she found the wet sponge sitting in the bottom of the sink one more time.

A breakthrough came for Jay one afternoon when Jeannine once again glared at him while she was holding the dripping sponge in her hand. Somehow, in that moment when he felt himself wanting to tell Jeannine off for once again being such a nag, he was able to stop for an instant and notice how Jeannine's disapproving look had sent him into a shame attack. He recognized his own impulse to attack with his angry words. But this time, instead of following that impulse, he was able to not follow the impulse to protect himself by striking out like a cornered animal. He felt himself wanting to protect in that way, but instead, taking what felt like a huge risk, he was able to say, "I feel like defending myself now, but I realize that I'm really feeling like I'm bad." He showed tremendous courage. His capacity for vulnerability stopped the usual argument right in its tracks.

Jeannine was also ultimately able to recognize her own part in "the saga of the sponge" dance. She began to see that whenever she saw the sponge sitting there in the sink, she was certain that Jay did not love her and, even closer to the core of her being, she felt that she was unlovable. Beneath what she viewed as Jay's disregard for her wishes around the sponge was a direct connection to her own sense of worthlessness. When Jay overlooked another of her requests around the house, Jeannine was able to notice her own familiar sense of being inherently unlovable. She, like Jay, was able to see that she had fallen into her own pit of shame, and that her reflex was to demand that Jay change his behavior. As each of them was more able to respond vulnerably when they felt hurt by the other, their intimacy began to grow.

This is not to say that in relationships we cannot ask each other to make alterations. Jay and Jeannine finally realized that Jeannine could request that the sponge get squeezed out. Now, most of the time, Jay remembers, understanding that this is an act of kindness for Jeannine. The sponge squeezing (or not) had to be liberated from the "I am bad" and "I am worthless and unlovable" stories of shame.

Liberation from Shame

At the end of the day, your liberation from shame must come from inside. This is an act of obtaining freedom. The steps toward that freedom cannot be taken by someone else, by waving a wand, or by some other kind of magic. They must be taken by you and you alone.

The balm you truly seek and need ultimately must be applied by compassion and tenderness for yourself—for the part of you that is still siding with the "I am bad" conclusion. This does not mean that your partner, your friends, your loved ones, even a stranger on the street cannot be a support to you in the meeting of your shame. We need each other. Our love and support for one another actually helps each of us take the internal leap into compassion. You, too, can finally begin to see that you do not have to destroy or obliterate your shame. In fact, you can't. However, your compassion has room for your shame; it encompasses it.

No one else can hold your shame compassionately for you. Even if your partner or someone else were able to say exactly what you think you want to hear, could tell you exactly the thing you think will erase your shame, the self-hatred you carry around will still be with you. You can't take someone else's shame away, no matter how much you care for them. What we can each do for one another is to hold a space of vulnerability and compassion (as much as possible) so the other can open their own heart of vulnerability and compassion.

When you are in the midst of a shame attack, sometimes you can find outside support, and sometimes not. When you can, it is a blessing. And when you can't, it can be a blessing as well. Finally, you can see that you actually have the capacity to compassionately welcome the bad, dark, unacceptable, and flawed beliefs you hold. You can vulnerably, tenderly, and lovingly hold the parts of you that you have concluded are unworthy of acceptance and belonging. You can begin to choose not to align with the domestication messages of "I am bad." Even if those aspects continue to feel unworthy of acceptance and belonging, you can hold the experience of unworthiness and unacceptability in the container of your vulnerable compassion. Once we are no longer children, the balm we long for does not ultimately come from the outside, but arises in our own vulnerability and compassion.

We cannot protect our partners from the pain of unworthiness and unacceptability, nor can they protect us. In relationships, we will inevitably do things big and small that cause our partner to spin into the grip of shame. When that happens, the potential is that we can be a witness, an example, and an inspiration for each other. Our leap into vulnerability, into compassion, is an inside job.

Exercise: Taking the Road Less Traveled

Set aside twenty to thirty minutes and find a spot where you can be alone and undisturbed. When you are ready to begin, think back to a recent time when your partner did or said something that was upsetting to you, that hurt you, or that annoyed you, a time when what your partner did and/or said caused you to feel something you did not want to feel. You may be thinking, "If my partner would just stop doing ________________________, then I would not have to feel ________________________." If that is what you are thinking, great. You are on the right track. The feeling that you do not want to be experiencing is likely to be the doorway to your path to shame.

For this exercise, we would like you to become very interested in how shame works inside of your system. Like a scientist performing an experiment, take your particular incident and play it over in your mind the way you might watch a movie. Recall the ways this plotline causes you to feel deficient. Again, just as an experiment, actually allow the story to send you down your road of shame. You may experience the belief that you are inherently bad or worthless or unredeemable or evil or defective or useless or broken or any other sort of deficiency that is the driver of your particular message of shame. As much as you can, go ahead and let yourself experience the full force of the shame.

Next, while imagining that you are the star of this movie of shame, see yourself taking full responsibility for whatever has occurred. You will never have to admit to another human being that you are taking this responsibility, but in this movie, you can. You have super powers of responsibility taking. In real life, you may have been afraid to take responsibility because you experience an internal imperative to avoid feeling that you are bad or worthless or unredeemable or evil or defective or useless or broken. But in this movie, with your super powers, you are able to see that although you have done something that you or someone else did not like, something that was off the mark, that was deficient, that could have been done oh-so-much better, you are not inherently flawed. You are simply imperfect.

Now, in this movie, you are able to experience your lack of perfection compassionately; you are able to allow yourself to suffer with your lack of perfection. Your heart is big enough to hold your imperfection. You may deeply regret a mistake, an action you have taken, but you are aware of your heart of compassion that does not require perfection. Deeply breathe into this cave of compassion that is a part of who you really are. You are always welcome here. Take as much time as you need before you move back into the normal activities of the rest of your day.

If at some point you would like to share your experience of this exercise with your partner, feel free to do so. It is not required, nor is your partner required to share his or her experience with you. The visit down this road of forgiveness, this road of compassion, this road less traveled, is for you.

CHAPTER SUMMARY

- The dynamics of shame and blame tend to be highly activated for both partners during the discovery, disclosure, and/or unraveling of one of the partner's acting out in a sexually compulsive way.
- Shame arises when you mistakenly associate unacceptable or "bad" with who you are inherently rather than simply with your actions. Internally, you have learned to believe you are a mistake.
- Blame is a familiar and handy tool for attempting to get rid of shame. It is easy to make the mistake (particularly with your intimate partner) of assuming that if you can just get him or her to stop doing whatever is annoying to you, then you will not have to feel the discomfort of shame.
- The antidote to shame is compassion for yourself first. Compassion arises when you allow yourself to be undefended, to be vulnerable, when you allow yourself to make friends with the uncomfortable feeling you are having.
- Your liberation from shame comes from inside. The balm you truly seek and need ultimately must be applied by compassion and tenderness for yourself—for the part of you that is siding with the "I am bad" conclusion.

Looking Forward

In Chapter 7, we will begin to look further at building vulnerability and compassion by developing your capacity for working with the strong feelings and emotions that are a part of dealing with any difficult issue.

CHAPTER 7

Working with Strong Feelings and Emotions

How can you move together as a couple from the wounded state of lack of connection and betrayal to the rewards available in relationship intimacy? The difficulties that have arisen in your relationship can lead to greater awareness and understanding and ultimately to a greater connection, but how? When your relationship has been broken by betrayal through sexual compulsivity, however the problem has manifested, no matter which side of the problem you are standing on, you are bound to be experiencing strong feelings and emotions.

Being able to tolerate and work through strong reactions and feelings of anger, fear, and pain can help both partners, as well as their relationship. These capacities and skills are not only fundamental to working with compulsive and addictive impulses, but also are steppingstones on your path to building greater intimacy.

Vulnerability and Intimacy

Humans are wired to need each other. So why is it that we seem to be unable to connect in ways that allow this basic need to be met? In relating with our closest partner, we have an opportunity to learn how to work with our strong feelings and emotions in ways that build vulnerability. This vulnerability is the key to unlocking the door to intimacy and connection.

To be vulnerable means you are willing to be hurt. If we emotionally block ourselves off from being hurt, we also shield ourselves from other feelings. We cannot selectively choose to only experience positive feelings and emotions and do away with the negative ones. If we banish fear, anger, and pain, we cut ourselves off from joy, love, and belonging.

We can be safe behind walls, but then we miss the wonders of visiting the ocean or skiing in the mountains or dining at a wonderful restaurant. In other words, we can give ourselves the illusion of the safety of walls, but at the high cost of walling ourselves off from connecting with others. We could wear a metal suit of armor, as if we were expecting to be called to joust at any moment, and we would feel protected, but the suit of armor would render us unable to feel the touch of others.

To inhibit our vulnerability is also to inhibit the physical and emotional touch of others. The armor makes us feel safer from the expected attacks of others, but at the price of vulnerability. To be sure, there is a place for armor and a place for vulnerability. Your most intimate relationship with your spouse is not the place for armor.

If we desire the rewards of the intimacy of human connection, then we must learn how to bare ourselves to the hurt, the wounding, that is also a part of our human interaction. In order to become vulnerable, we need to learn to work with our survival impulses that urge us to fight, flee, or freeze when faced with what we perceive as potential danger. We need to learn how to negotiate our most primitive human emotions. We need to see that the experience of these emotions will not destroy us. Then, we can learn how to build the emotional muscles needed to be vulnerable.

Heather and Bryan Visit "Instinctive-Reactive World"

When our intimate sexual connection is betrayed, the hurt, anger, and fear that arise can be intense. When faced with a conflict, most of us tend to look to the outside to see what is causing our negative feelings. This is a normal human reaction—an instinct, even.

To show how this mechanism works, let's look at an example not charged with the elements of sex and betrayal. Hopefully, this method of showing the dynamic won't cause your protective flags of blame and/or shame to surface.

We first talked about Heather and Bryan in Chapter 4. Bryan, you may recall, sought support for his compulsion to view Internet porn. Bryan was able to see that his attraction to and use of porn was actually preventing the closeness he so wanted to have with Heather. He and Heather both began to see how seemingly everyday misunderstandings can lead to the same kind of impulse for protection from shame and vulnerability (as well as avoidance of strong feelings and emotions) that sent Bryan to his computer looking for more porn. They both committed to building their skills of vulnerability to deepen their connection and intimacy.

Bryan and Heather were getting married, and had engagement photos taken. Their arrangement was that they would each pay for half of the photos. Heather was supposed to write a check for her half of the cost and leave it on the kitchen counter so Bryan could deliver both checks to the photographer the next day. But Heather forgot to write her check.

The next morning when Bryan went to the kitchen counter, there was no check. He immediately felt annoyed. He felt that he had been wronged. Heather had said she would write the check, and she did not. He wasn't fully aware that a whole string of assumptions had begun to flow. Instantly, he was certain that he was in the right. Heather had said she would write the check. He had suggested she do it the moment they discussed it, and she didn't. He began to think that Heather was being selfish, or she must not really respect him or love him.

By the time Heather called Bryan on her lunch break that day, she had remembered that she had forgotten to write the check. When she called, she said, "Hi, how are you doing?" Bryan, in a peeved voice, said, "Hey, you forgot to leave the check." Heather then became irritated with Bryan's tone, and replied, "This is why I don't like to call you on my lunch break. You just give me a hard time instead of being happy to hear from me." This further angered Bryan, and he hung up on Heather. Bryan and Heather had both entered "instinctive-reactive world." This is the place where you instinctively react to the annoying things your partner says or does. Does that sound familiar?

This dynamic goes on all the time. An event occurs that causes you to feel something, and that something feels bad. You might not even totally realize it feels bad because often you quickly justify the bad feeling with the fact that you are in the right. In this case, Bryan interpreted Heather's actions in a way that he felt hurt.

When Heather called Bryan at lunchtime, she assumed that Bryan's irritated tone was a rejection of her. She didn't know that he had misinterpreted her mistake of forgetting to write the check. From the hurt that Heather experienced in feeling scolded by Bryan, she lashed back with her angry comment. She also felt justified in her position. She had made a mistake; she had simply forgotten to do something. She felt that she was being unjustly reprimanded, and that felt bad.

What happened to Bryan and Heather in instinctive-reactive world is similar to what happened with Jeannine and Jay and the infamous saga of the sponge in Chapter 6. Underneath the automatic response of anger was hurt. In Chapter 6, the focus was on the blame and shame mechanism. In this chapter, we're noticing when you react to situations on automatic pilot. As you build your skill of being able to tolerate your strong feelings and emotions, you will become more effective in recognizing how your strong feelings and emotions can set the shame-blame cycle into motion.

The Marshmallow Test

In the early 1970s, Stanford professor Walter Mischel conducted a famous experiment with four- to six-year-olds around the mechanism of delayed gratification. Each child was given one marshmallow and told that if they could resist eating the one marshmallow until the researcher returned about fifteen minutes later, they could have two marshmallows. Most of the kids ate the marshmallow before the experimenter came back into the room, many of them right away. Only one-third of the kids could resist eating the marshmallow prior to the experimenter's return.

When Mischel followed up ten (and then twenty) years later, he found that the now-grown individuals who had been able to resist eating the marshmallow were highly correlated with individuals who had higher SAT scores, more successful marriages, higher incomes, and generally more fulfilling lives.

So what can you do to build the skill of resisting so that you can reap the rewards of the delayed gratification? How do you learn to work with your instinctive impulses? Are you doomed to remain the subject of your impulse to move against, away from, or toward?

Let's say that you were one of the kids who ate the marshmallow right away. Does this mean that you are condemned to a less fulfilling life than the marshmallow-resisting youngsters? No. We are certain that you can build the mechanism of delaying gratification, of working with your strong feelings and emotions.

We have watched ourselves and others learn to work with the impulses of pain, anger, and fear that propel us into actions that alienate us from the connection with our partner we ultimately desire. We have seen ourselves and others learn to build the muscle of resisting the one marshmallow for the reward of intimacy that comes with the prefrontal capacity to make choices, reconcile conflicting thoughts, process emotions, suppress urges, and delay immediate gratification.

Developing a New Capacity

To be no longer terrorized by fear, anger, and pain is a pivotal movement. We have found that the capacity to fully allow these feelings is actually a long-term (possibly a lifetime) project. When you recognize your response as a survival impulse, you can make an informed choice about how you will respond to the impulse. If you are actually in danger, you will respond accordingly. But if not, you can make a better choice than to give into your automatic impulse.

In the context of intimate relationships, you are instinctively equating the uncomfortable or negative feeling you are experiencing with danger, but there is no actual emergency. This is an important place to start. What happened to Bryan when he looked on the kitchen counter and saw there was no check? If this was a movie and we could internally slow the scenes down and look at what was happening frame by frame, here is what we might see:

Bryan quickly and without thinking interpreted Heather's lack of action as an affront to him—a lack of respect, a lack of love. Instantly, he experienced hurt, then, just as quickly, he experienced irritation (anger). In the next instant, he believed that Heather was responsible for his anger; if she really loved and respected him, she would have written that check, After all, he had even reminded her to do it.

In your ordinary day-to-day awareness, it is difficult to slow yourself down to notice what is going on internally frame by frame. Your reactions occur so quickly that they can be difficult to recognize. Sometimes, you have a moment for thought. For example, Bryan had a thought about Heather not caring for him. But sometimes your reaction is purely reflexive, and you cannot banish it. Even so, you can begin to recognize that you are having the survival response. The feeling of anger, fear, or pain, of entering the cycle of shame-blame, can become a signal to pay attention. Once you have taken that very important step of paying attention and becoming consciously aware of your automatic response, it is no longer automatic. Then you can make a conscious choice about how to respond.

The Road to Developing Vulnerability and Intimacy

How can you unblock your capacity to be empathic and vulnerable so that you can experience the intimacy and joy of human connection? How can you bring greater awareness, and through this greater awareness build vulnerability and true intimacy? If your anger, fear, and pain are natural impulses, what can you do when you feel them? You can learn to build your capacity for choice and decision making in a way that overrides your instinctive impulses.

You can use the thinking part of your brain to label and evaluate the rush of your biochemical response. Building such skills not only increases your capacity for intimacy, it helps you work with compulsive, addictive impulses. This sounds very simple, and actually, it is. But first you need to believe that you can do it.

In a very simple form, the basic steps on the road to developing vulnerability and intimacy are:

1. Recognize your instinctive response for what it is.
2. Allow yourself to experience the feeling without indulging or repressing.
3. From this place of inner vulnerability, choose to take action or not.

Step One: Recognize Your Instinctive Responses

First, you must be able to recognize when you are having a survival impulse. Then you can experience the underlying feeling. This process is exactly what is meant in the admonition to "count to three" when you feel angry. You try to recognize that you are having an instinctive response of fear, anger, or pain, and then just feel that feeling. This works as a delaying tactic so that the slightly slower part of your brain—the thinking part—has a chance to show up.

Your impulses of fear, anger, and pain immediately compel you to pay attention. As you begin to become more skillful in recognizing that you are having (or have had) an instinctive response, you can let these responses become your allies. You can bring more awareness and consciousness into your life.

Start by simply telling yourself that you are going to start noticing your instantaneous responses of fear, anger, and pain. The strong intention to notice the flare-ups (even the very tiny impulses) of your instinctive response will build awareness.

Another way is by thinking back to a moment of feeling unsafe in some way, and then recalling your instant and instinctive response. In our example of Bryan reacting to Heather not remembering to write the check, the moment Bryan looked at the kitchen counter and did not see her check he experienced a feeling of annoyance. Just to be clear, we are not suggesting that Bryan stop his feeling of anger. In fact, he can't. We are suggesting that he become aware that he's experiencing anger (irritation)—in that moment or as soon as he can—and simply see it for what it is. Then the angry response can become a signal that has his attention.

When you have an experience that you are instinctively labeling as painful, uncomfortable, bad, your survival impulses become activated. It's similar to when the doctor hits your knee with the little rubber hammer. If your reflexes are operating properly, without any thought on your part, your leg just kicks right out.

Does this mean that you are doomed to reactivity? Luckily, you are not, because you also have a thinking part to your human brain. The dilemma we all face is that the more primitive animal part of our biology creates automatic impulses that fire off quickly.

The Good News Within the Bad News

We've heard it said that automatic unconscious responses will continue as long as you have a body. While this might sound like bad news, recognizing this truth is actually the good news. If you know that your survival impulses are going to continue to fire up, creating responses of fear, anger, and pain, you can finally cut yourself some slack. You can begin to work with your responses so you don't remain like a rat in a maze, subject to the internal, eternal firings of your survival mechanisms.

You are the ruler of the dominion of your body, emotions, and feelings. You can be a benevolent ruler or you can be a tyrant. A tyrant attempts to banish his or her feelings of fear, anger, and pain. A benevolent ruler recognizes that an impulsive response is merely that—an impulsive response.

The Value of Your Instinctive Responses

Still, you would not want to eliminate your fight, flight, and freezing responses even if you could. They are part of your survival mechanisms that help when your life or the lives of those around you are in danger. These responses provide all of us with information that is a part of natural intelligence.

Paldrom was walking home late one night when she was living in New York City. She was almost home, and there was no one else she could see on the dimly lit street. Suddenly, a tall, thin, dark man stepped out of the shadows and grabbed her arm from behind and swung her around. Without any kind of thought, she automatically raised the empty metal cookie tin she was carrying, as if to hit the guy. Her lip literally snarled, and she growled, "Leave me alone." The guy ran away. Trembling, Paldrom saw a cab turn onto the street, and she stopped it to report what had just happened. In that moment, Paldrom was extremely happy that her survival impulse to fight had done its job.

We have all heard stories about people having the strength and courage to lift a car off a child who was trapped, being able to escape from a burning building, heroically responding to attack in times of battle. These are all the benefits received from healthy survival impulses, and they are an important part of your human biology. They are signals that give you vital information. Without the native intelligence provided by your emotional impulses, your more highly evolved thinking processes don't have a basis from which to work.

You don't want to banish your emotional impulses. However, when your instinctive responses are creating difficulty, such as when they are leading you into a cycle of compulsive behavior, it can be helpful to learn how to work with them effectively.

Step Two: Experience Your Instinctive Responses

You don't want to and can't rid yourself of the knee-jerk responses of your protective intuition. It does no good to go to war internally with these impulses. But when they cause you to act addictively or in ways that keep you from achieving the human connection you so deeply desire, you need a plan, a way to skillfully work with these natural impulses.

Your closest intimate relationship is the place these negative feelings can come up most frequently and strongly. Since your relationship is the place in which these impulses are arising, your relationship can and must be the very place to work with them.

So how can you more deeply allow your instinctive responses to connect with your reasoning responses? How can you more effectively build the bridge between your instinctive impulse and the more reasoning executive function?

Building the Bridge

Bridging your impulses with your reason is a skill you can develop by allowing yourself to simply and fully experience your feelings. You are attempting to build increased capacity (like the kids who could resist the one marshmallow) so you can gain the rewards that come from making choices, reconciling conflicting thoughts, processing emotions, suppressing urges, and delaying immediate gratification.

In an instant of recognizing that you are experiencing a difficult, uncomfortable, even excruciating feeling or emotion, first check to see if you are actually in danger. If you are not, take a slow deep breath and relax. Do not resist or protect yourself. Let go. Be patient with yourself in this practice. Like anything else, it can take a while to get the hang of it. And even once you begin to develop an understanding and capacity to let go, new and perhaps more subtle incidents that trigger your protector impulses will appear. We have found that the tenacity of the protective instinctive messages to fight, flee, and/or freeze can at times seem to be relentless. The more you are able to make friends with these aspects of your inner functioning, the more you can work with them.

For example, let's revisit the situation with Bryan and the forgotten check. A good start for Bryan was simply being able to recognize that he was feeling justified. He could see that the "justified" story he was telling himself was woven with righteousness. This recognition of righteousness was a clue to look to what those feelings might be covering. In an instant, he understood that he was actually feeling irritated, and beneath the irritation, he was feeling hurt.

Some people have compared meeting anger, fear, and pain to baring themselves to the rain or diving into the ocean. One lovely description we heard was from a young woman who described it as first stilling her thoughts, and then imagining the space in between the cells of her body. She reported that the uncomfortable waves of emotion had all the space they needed to rage and be free right between her cells. All that force of strong feeling and emotion became a passing wave of energy.

One man described this letting go as similar to playing in the waves at the ocean. He said, "If you fight the wave, it takes you down, but if you dive into the wave, you can ride it." It is possible to turn and face, to welcome, the very impulse your instinctive biology is urging you to avoid. The instinctive impulse comes more quickly, but the ability to recognize the impulse for what it is isn't built with greater effort but with greater openness. Being vulnerable is often equated with a sense of letting go.

Avoiding Your Impulses by Indulging Them

If you are like most of us, even when you are able to recognize that you are having a flash of instinctive anger, fear, or emotional pain, you will also feel a strong impulse to do something to get away from the feeling or to get the feeling away from you. You may notice a tendency to attempt to banish your feelings, to avoid them, to deny them, to repress them, or to indulge them by acting on the impulse.

Indulging is simply following the instinctive imperative of the feeling. For example, if you feel angry, an instinctive response would be to yell at someone or to kick something. If you feel afraid, your instinct will tell you to run away or freeze up. If you feel hurt, you might cry. It is normal to cry, to feel pain, to say, "Ouch, stop it" when you are hurt. However, if you find yourself thinking the same painful thought over and over again or repeatedly feeling the same unpleasant reactive response to a particular incident, this is a clue that you are literally in an instinctive mental or emotional spin.

You can begin to recognize that any of the responses of acting against, running away, or internally spinning are simply various ways that we as humans indulge the instinctive imperative. Indulging is a form of avoidance, rather than simply letting go and experiencing the uncomfortable feeling.

To allow yourself to notice and experience your anger, fear, and pain does not mean taking those feelings and throwing them at your partner with the explanation, "I'm only telling you how I feel." That would not be an expression of vulnerability and will not lead to greater intimacy. In the next chapter, we discuss more fully developing the skill of speaking to your partner vulnerably by telling the truth about your experience using the skill of undefended honesty. And in Chapter 10, you will find instructions on developing your skills of intimate communication.

For now, remember that in a moment when you are able to notice that you are in reaction, when you are feeling the impulse to fight, flee, or spin with the same thought or emotion over and over, this is your opportunity to pause. You can begin to recognize that your first impulse to something that registers as dangerous or threatening (even if it is not) is more than likely going to be a survival reaction. Speaking your angry feelings coupled with the exclamation, "This is just how I feel," is creating an excuse for indulging rather than directly experiencing.

Repressing Your Feelings by Numbing Them

To compensate for unwelcome feelings, many people use numbing diversions. This compensatory numbing activity can become a conditioned response put in place as a strategy to avoid the unwanted feelings. Many things, both positive and negative, can be used to numb—work, exercise, alcohol, drugs, food, and, of course, compulsive sexual activity. However, if you allow the uncomfortable feelings of anger, fear, and pain to become your allies, the uncomfortable impulses become signals indicating, "Attention needed here." If you can view these impulses as signals, then you do not need to employ the harmful strategies of attempting to get away from them.

In the case of compulsive urges, an individual may use the compulsive behavior to avoid feeling the full impact of the anger, fear, or pain. This sets up the addictive-compulsive cycle. Being able to experience the rush of information being sent by the impulse allows you to go to the next step of taking action (or not) or speaking (or not). From the less reactive place that is not in avoidance, you are vulnerable. And from this vulnerability you can build the intimacy that you truly desire.

Your Patterns of Avoidance

Most of us have built habits of avoidance. You probably began these habits when you were quite young. It can sometimes be helpful to track back and find the seeds of your avoidant strategies. In Chapter 9, we will look at how to do that and how this tracking back skill has helped others. While it can be useful, you are not required to trace your impulses back into the past. In an instant, you can simply stop and experience an uncomfortable impulse. In that instant, you will find that it wasn't such a monster after all. Before you allow the impulse, though, if you are like most of us, the anger, fear, or pain that is chasing you can disguise itself as a monster. How else could this survival impulse do its job of getting your attention?

You may begin to recognize that you have spent much of your lifetime running from sensations of fear, anger, and pain. Many have reported the relief of finally turning and facing the internal monster. In the *The Wizard of Oz*, when Toto revealed the man behind the curtain, the wizard could no longer use his tricks to scare Dorothy and her friends. When a child is afraid of a monster under the bed or in the closet, the skillful parent does not pooh-pooh the child's fear, but acknowledges the fear and helps the child check it out.

In this way, you can skillfully work with yourself with compassion, by acknowledging the capacity you have had all along (like Dorothy with her ruby slippers in *The Wizard of Oz*) to directly and simply bear the discomfort of your innate intuitive protective response.

Recognizing That You Are Meeting the Painful Experience

How can you recognize that you have actually experienced the uncomfortable feeling? Is there a sign or a clue? Yes, there is. You know that you have really met the uncomfortable impulse because the biochemical instinctive response will change. This is important. You will know that you have brought awareness to the biological impulse because your experience will be different from what it was previously.

In the moment of opening, of letting go, the uncomfortable feeling may not be obliterated. You may still be experiencing it—or not. However, in the openness of vulnerability, the uncomfortable reaction is not resisted and can be fully experienced. The compassion of vulnerability has the capacity to contain the discomfort.

If you find yourself thinking the same thing over and over again, feeling the same feeling over and over again, justifying why you are thinking and feeling the same thing over and over again, blaming your partner for making you feel this bad thing over and over again, you can skillfully take that recognition as a clue. The "over and over again" experience is probably an impulse of anger, fear, or pain that you are avoiding.

In general, if you are feeling angry, afraid, or hurt for an extended period of time, it is useful to check and see if you may be circling around the actual feeling and not allowing the wisdom of your thinking brain to tolerate the discomfort of your anger, fear, or pain response. By avoiding the discomfort, you can drag the uncomfortable feeling on indefinitely.

Some people spend a lifetime feeling the same experience of anger, fear, or pain over and over again. They may associate the feeling with an unending parade of events and circumstances, but the feeling is never fully met and experienced.

It is important to note that grief has a long-term signature. This means that grief will come back again and again, in a way that anger, fear, pain, or hurt does not. Grief, a response to a shock, must unwind. It requires you to be patient and allow the unwinding of the pain of the loss to go on for as long as it takes. Generally, a spark of anger, fear, and hurt is more of a momentary flash meant to get your attention instantly.

Once you have met a strong, uncomfortable impulse of anger, fear, or pain, don't trick yourself into believing this means it will never come back. It will. You, too, are human and will continue to be the beneficiary of the information available from the instinctive messages of your anger, fear, and pain. As you learn to ride these particular waves, however, you will develop the capacity to relate more vulnerably than protectively.

Step Three: Make a Choice from Vulnerability

Once you notice that you are experiencing the imperative to fight, flee, or freeze, you can then make a choice about how you would actually like to respond. You must be willing to directly experience the impulsive feelings you are having. This willingness is the birth of vulnerability. The impulse to fight, flee, or freeze is not being vulnerable; it is protective. Vulnerability is the antidote to the impulse to protect; vulnerability is the basis of creating intimacy first with yourself and then with your partner.

Reflecting on his interaction with Heather, Bryan realized that the irritation he was feeling (and the righteous indignation that accompanied it) was a signal. He could then review and realize that the irritation he had felt was covering up feeling hurt. He was vulnerable enough with himself to recognize the hurt. Because he did not feel that he needed to shield himself from the feeling of hurt, he no longer felt the need to accuse Heather. She had indeed done something that had hurt him, but her intention was not to wound.

When an uncomfortable impulse arises and you are able to recognize it and then experience it without indulging or repressing, greater clarity will be available to you. Remember, you are not meeting the uncomfortable feeling to rid yourself of it. That only creates greater resistance internally. It may help to imagine that you are meeting the uncomfortable feeling to partake of it more fully, to understand it more deeply. Some people have been helped by the image of inviting the uncomfortable impulse to tea. Once the meeting occurs, as we mentioned earlier, your experience of the uncomfortable emotion will be altered. Since you are no longer in avoidance, you become vulnerable.

Vulnerability in Action

Going back once again to the check incident (or shall we say the lack-of-check incident) between Bryan and Heather, when Bryan was able to recognize that he was in reaction, he could simply stop and track his first response of irritation, and recognize it as a cover-up of his feeling of hurt.

That night when Heather and Bryan arrived home from work, Bryan was able to tell Heather that he was sorry he had gotten irritated about the check. He was able to vulnerably share with Heather that he'd realized he had fallen into a moment of hurt because he felt like she didn't really care for him. This vulnerability on Bryan's part made Heather smile. She said, "Yeah, I'm sorry I forgot to write the check. I can be such a space cadet about things like that, huh? Sorry I got mad at you when I called at lunch."

The other part of this story involves Heather's realization about her reaction on the phone. There is a good reason that she was able to apologize as well. That afternoon as she was working, Heather experienced first her own righteousness because she "didn't do anything wrong." She felt anger toward Bryan for hanging up on her. By allowing the anger to wash through her without holding on to the story of her righteousness, she was able to experience the pain of feeling bad for being "imperfect," because she had let Bryan down by forgetting to write the check. She could see how she had internally leapt to the conclusion that his anger with her meant that he didn't really care for her.

As they were able to talk vulnerably, both could pretty quickly come to the point of being amused that they both had ended up with the conclusion that the other did not really care. The potential is that either partner or both can back out of "reactive world" by experiencing the uncomfortable feeling and then allowing the more thinking function to be in charge of the communication. We have often said to each other, "If just one of us can stay sane in any given moment (that is, not trapped by our reactive strategies), then we at least have a chance at vulnerability, intimacy, and truly connecting."

It May Not Be Easy, but It's Worth It

Compassion for yourself during this process is vital. You are working with a protective system that is hard-wired into your body. Some of us are more sensitive, more reactive, than others. Some of us are more prone to choosing compulsive strategies than others. But we are certain that if you have the capacity to read this book, you have the capacity to bear the discomfort of your anger, fear, and pain responses and bring greater vulnerability into your life. The rewards of building the capacity to make choices, to reconcile conflicting thoughts, to process emotions, to suppress urges, to delay immediate gratification are greater joy, love, and belonging as well as greater vulnerability. We have personally seen how the process of meeting what arises in your relationship may always be challenging, but the intimacy that it brings is ultimately and infinitely rewarding.

Exercise: Shaping Clay

For this exercise, you will need two large handfuls of modeling clay, one handful for each partner.

Put your blob of clay on the table in front of you, and with your thumbs, press as hard as you can into the clay. You will find that the clay resists your penetration.

Now, instead of pressing as hard as you can, press gently, applying constant gentle but firm pressure. You will begin to feel the clay begin to melt beneath your thumbs. The clay will let you into its core.

Allow the experience of feeling the clay yielding beneath your touch to be a metaphor, a direct experience of how you can actually allow yourself to melt, to not resist, at the moment of an instinctive impulse to fight, flee, or seduce, but instead to become vulnerable. We recognize how difficult it can be to resist those instinctive, protective urges. Let the experience of the clay giving way to your gentle pressure begin to create new pathways in your awareness that open up a possibility you may not have been able to find before.

CHAPTER SUMMARY

- Being able to tolerate and work with your strong reactions and feelings of anger, fear, and pain is not only fundamental to working with compulsive and addictive impulses but also to building greater intimacy.
- If we desire the rewards of intimate human connection, then we must learn to bare ourselves to the hurt, the wounding, that is also a part of our human interaction.

- You can't (and don't want to) banish your reactive impulses of anger, fear, or pain. However, when your instinctive responses are creating difficulty, such as when they lead to a cycle of compulsive behavior, it is helpful to learn how to work with these impulses effectively.
- You can learn to build your capacity for choice and decision making in ways that override your instant and instinctive impulses. Once you have taken the very important step of becoming consciously aware of your automatic response, you have the opportunity to make a conscious choice about how to respond.
- The basic steps of using the thinking brain to evaluate and work with the rush of your biological impulses of anger, fear, and pain are:

  1. Recognize your instinctive response for what it is.
  2. Allow yourself to experience the feeling without indulging or repressing.
  3. From this place of inner vulnerability, choose to take action or not.

Looking Forward

In Chapter 8, we will begin the investigation of how the capacity to work with your strong feelings and emotions can aid you in deepening your relationship by developing the skill of undefended honesty.

CHAPTER 8

Undefended Honesty

Working with couples who have faced the challenge of rebuilding a relationship that has been injured by sex addiction, we have found a common denominator among those couples who are able to build an even stronger and deeper relationship. These individuals have built their skill and capacity for what we refer to as undefended honesty. This is an honesty that builds on the truth that has been revealed in the disclosure of the sexually compulsive behavior. This kind of honesty is not easy or natural to do, nor is it necessarily easy or natural to receive. But these skills can be developed. This chapter provides a roadmap of the land of undefended honesty.

The partner who has acted out sexually (in whatever way) needs to build his skill at telling the truth about his compulsive behavior. As mentioned earlier, this can be difficult due to the shame factor. Shame leads to the desire to cover up, which leads to lying—outright false statements and lies of omission.

Let the challenge of this difficulty motivate you to find ways to know what you are thinking and feeling and to communicate those thoughts and feelings more effectively. The partner of the sexually compulsive individual also benefits from building her skills of undefended honesty. As the partner of someone who is acting out sexually, she may fall into the trap of focusing on remedying her partner's compulsion to the detriment of her own wishes and desires. Even though this urge to rescue her partner may arise from a noble motivation, it does not work—for either party involved.

A relationship is a meeting of two partners who can support themselves and provide support for each other. If you do not take care of yourself first, you will not be able to be useful to anyone else. This is not a selfish stance, but a compassionate one. In this chapter, we are encouraging you to take care of yourself and your relationship by deeply, vulnerably, and radically showing up and telling the truth. Again, this may be easy to say but challenging to do.

Why Accept the Challenge of Undefended Honesty?

The impulse to lie is generally an impulse to avoid pain or seek pleasure, to get away from what you don't want or to get what you do want in any given moment. We all have this impulse; it's part of our survival mechanism. We all know about the kid with his hand in the cookie jar telling his mom that he's not taking any cookies—guilty and denying it simultaneously. The problem with denial and lying is that the first person to sense that you are not telling the truth is you.

Sometimes, not telling the truth is exactly what is required to protect ourselves, our loved ones, our community. We are not speaking here about distinctions regarding the morality of telling the truth or lying. We are pointing to the direct benefits you can receive from practicing undefended honesty. This level of honesty is necessary for your relationship with yourself and for your relationship with your partner. Ultimately, undefended honesty can become a cornerstone of rebuilding the trust in your relationship. But let's start by investigating how undefended honesty is foundational in building internal compassion.

The Importance of Undefended Honesty for You

We have found that both partners benefit from investigating whatever it is they have been hiding from themselves. But the one person who needs your undefended honesty the most is you. Your mind, your being, longs for acceptance. To the extent that you're denying, you're not accepting. You may think you are protecting yourself or shielding yourself from having to look at what you have determined is "ugly." The denial of that not-so-pretty part of yourself is a seed of self-hatred. You can't have compassion for something while denying that it exists. The denial that something you are thinking and feeling is not there doesn't make it not there. If an elephant is charging at you, you can close your eyes, but the elephant is still going to run you down.

We have all been taught in one way or another that some of what we think and feel is unacceptable. By believing that, we deny ourselves the direct experience of who we are—in effect, we lie to ourselves.

In Chapter 7, we investigated the mechanism of directly experiencing the information arising from our internal impulses—even the negative or painful feelings and emotions. It is one thing to work with a painful feeling or emotion because we are directly aware of it. It is quite another to allow ourselves to uncover thoughts, feelings, and emotions that we don't want to have to admit exist. It requires a leap of courage to look to thoughts, feelings, and emotions that have been labeled "do not enter" or "do not disturb"—the ones that we have learned good boys or good girls do not think or feel.

We are not suggesting indulgence of your impulses or acting anything out. We are merely pointing to the compassionate act of telling the truth to yourself, to ceasing the judgment that does not allow you to admit (at least to yourself) what you are actually thinking and feeling.

Recall any instance in your life in which you were truly honest with yourself (even if you did not like what you found) and we suspect you will remember a moment of relief. That experience of relief is the balm of compassion that comes with letting go of the defense. For example, imagine holding your hand in a tight fist until it begins to ache, then allowing your hand to open. There is a relief in the act of simply letting go.

In addition to the sense of liberation you will feel, telling the undefended truth begins to strip away a layer of defense. It can be painful to give up your armor, but it is also painful to walk around with all that weight of protection. It can feel as if admitting to something that you feel shame about would be the last thing in the world you want to do. It may seem like walking off a ledge. But there is relief in the freefall of telling the truth.

You do not necessarily need to share the truth you tell to yourself with anyone else; the power of simply telling the truth internally provides relief from the pressure of the walled-up denial of the thoughts and feelings you learned were somehow unacceptable. Again, as we mentioned earlier, we aren't advocating for the acting out of any feeling. We are talking about not indulging and not repressing. We are pointing to nakedly admitting to yourself what you (as a human with the reactions of a mind and body) are experiencing.

That letting go, that undefended honesty with yourself, builds your capacity to tell the truth to yourself again and again. It leads not only to greater compassion for yourself, but for everyone else as well. If you have greater compassion and acceptance for yourself, you can extend that to others—and specifically to your relationship with your intimate partner.

Charlie Finally Tells the Truth to Himself

Charlie had a problem with his temper. In his initial work with us, he began to see how for years of his life he had chosen to live alone, masturbating while looking at porn rather than risk being in a relationship with a live, flesh-and-blood woman who might disappoint him and whom he might disappoint. He eventually met and married a woman who ran her own small business as a graphic designer, but their relationship was troubled. Charlie would fly into a rage and scream at his wife when he felt she was unavailable to him or when he felt she was disapproving.

His wife would periodically stay up at night working on her graphic design projects, particularly when she had a big project with an imminent deadline. When Charlie would wake up in the night and find that his wife was not in bed with him, he would often feel an instant sense of abandonment. And then, just as quickly, he would begin his line of reasoning about how his wife was working too much, was irresponsible in her time management, how she did not care for him, and how he could not stand to remain in a marriage with someone who really did not care for him. He would then come into the room where his wife was working away and begin to berate her for being a bad wife. As you can imagine, these conversations did not go very well.

Finally, one night Charlie woke up and watched himself begin to feel those old familiar feelings of abandonment, of not being cared for. He had investigated his history enough to recognize that these feelings were the same feelings he had felt when he came home from school and found his mother in the dining room with one of her friends, drinking, and oblivious to the fact that he had even walked in the door. In the moment of that remembering, he could tell the truth to himself about where these feelings were coming from. He let the content of those thoughts of abandonment melt like butter in the hot sun. That was step one. And a very good first step. He began to tell the undefended truth to himself. He recognized that he was telling himself a story of abandonment. This did not stop his experience of abandonment, of course. The story, the feelings, were still coming to get him. But he did something he had never done before. Instead of walking into the room where his wife was working and yelling at her, he walked into the room and vulnerably told her the undefended truth.

It was hard for him as a grown man to show his wife that he was having the experience of a young boy and actually just wanted comfort. He had to override the impulse he was having that told him that if he talked about these feelings, if he revealed them, that he would be crushed, and that he would be judged as childish and inferior.

For as long as he could remember, he had not allowed these feelings to see the light of day. To do so would have meant admitting to himself that he was weak. These thoughts and feelings seemed so ugly and selfish. He could remember being told to "be a big boy." He did not want to have needs, and if he did, he certainly did not want them showing because that would mean that he was deficient. So he had lashed out instead. He had felt like if he just acted as if he was the boss, the man, that he could demand what he needed.

His feelings were so tender and embarrassing to him that the best he could do was walk into the room where his wife was working and say, "I'm feeling panicky and angry. I want to blame you. I can't see straight in this moment. Help." As you can probably imagine, this undefended moment of truth telling elicited an entirely different response from his wife than the angry outbursts of accusation. She stopped what she was doing and said, "Come here. Tell me what is going on." They sat down on the sofa and he put his head on her shoulder. She tenderly rubbed his head while he allowed himself to experience the pain of feeling so utterly unloved. His wife was not fixing this pain for him, but she was helping him create an environment where he could tell the truth about it in an undefended way. This was not the last time Charlie woke up in the night with a sense of abandonment, but the spell of defense had been broken by his undefended honesty.

Working with Compulsive Behaviors

As we discussed in Chapter 6, the addictive cycle is fueled by the despair of shame. You may have a natural knee-jerk, lie-telling response to avoid the hopeless feeling of shame. You may tell yourself you do not really feel out of control and powerless, when actually you do. This lying to yourself feeds the addictive cycle of: 1) a preoccupation with the perceived need; 2) a routine that leads up to the compulsive behavior; 3) engaging in the compulsive behavior; and finally, 4) the despair of shame that leads back to the beginning of the cycle with further preoccupation with the perceived need.

We have found that undefended, rigorous honesty is at the core of working with any type of compulsive behavior. If you look closely, you will discover that honesty opens the door to overcoming compulsion or addiction. Some have even dubbed honesty with oneself as the "Step Zero" of the Twelve Steps (see Chapter 11). That's how fundamental honesty is in meeting compulsivity. Being honest with yourself is the foundation, the key to working with the addictive cycle. It is also the key to working with shame and blame, to accepting your strong feelings and emotions, and to creating a foundation for rebuilding your relationship.

Honesty for Your Relationship

In order to rebuild your relationship, you need to rebuild trust. In order to rebuild trust, you must commit to undefended honesty. In a relationship with another, each time you experience honesty from your partner (and time confirms that your partner has indeed told the truth), your trust grows. In the absence of honesty—in fact, in the absence of information or the lie of omission—the partner who has experienced being lied to will fill in the blanks with the imagination of past actions based on history. If the past history includes deception and betrayal, that is what she will use to fill in the blanks.

Your relationship has its own life. There are the two partners, and then there is also the combined energy of the partners. As in the synergist wisdom that speaks to the sum being greater than the individual parts, the combination of the wisdom of both partners can create a knowingness that would otherwise not be available. This new intelligence is born through meeting difficulty and is fostered by the capacity for undefended truth telling. A key to overcoming a time of crisis in a relationship is for both partners to have the willingness to tell the truth (at least to themselves) about whatever it is they are thinking, feeling, perceiving. This can be tricky because, as mentioned earlier, we can hide the truth from ourselves about the parts of us that we feel are wrong, bad, or otherwise unacceptable. As discussed in Chapter 6, it is much easier to move into blaming your partner than to stir the monster of internal shame.

Being honest with your partner can actually show how much you care about him or her. The act of undefended and vulnerable sharing with your beloved is like exposing a precious and tender part of yourself. Intimacy invites the sharing of the good in you so your partner can also enjoy it. Exposing your flaws, your "bad" parts, can be a gift, too, because, by not hiding them, they will not be hidden deceptions waiting to come out later to create chaos and hurt. It is the journey of a hero to expose your flaws, to lay your cards on the table, to resist the impulse to defend and protect by telling a lie or attempting to hide.

Making a Safe Place for the Truth

We've all had moments of listening to someone's explanations and having a sense that the person was not being truthful or, perhaps, not fully truthful. In courtroom scenes, we hear the words, "the truth, the whole truth, and nothing but the truth." But what can you do if your spouse is not telling the whole truth and nothing but the truth?

What you don't want to do is be a prosecutor, a judge, or a jury. That is not your role. What you can do is try to make it safe for your partner to tell the truth. The person on the witness stand in a legal drama who does not tell the whole truth is typically afraid of something, such as revealing guilt. The intention behind not telling the truth is often fear.

How can you make it safer and less fearful for your partner to tell the truth? One way you can do that is by being clear that your job is not to prove that they are lying or not telling the whole truth. Your job is to make it safe for your partner to admit the truth. To that end, your partner needs to believe that you want to hear the truth, not as an indictment, but for the purposes of building trust in the relationship.

When you are open and vulnerable, and you allow the other person to express himself or herself in an open and vulnerable way, relationship trust can grow. We recognize that you may feel that, given what has previously occurred regarding sexually compulsive behavior, trust in the relationship may seem ill advised and, if even possible, thousands of miles away from where you are now. However, it is possible; it is recommended. In fact, sharing truths creates intimacy. You have probably had a direct experience of this when someone trusted you enough to tell you a personal secret.

How to Work with Undefended Honesty

We all have negative qualities. These negative qualities are also often referred to as the "shadow." They are the qualities you try to keep out of the light of awareness, and certainly out of sight of your beloved partner.

A folktale tells of a man so frightened by his own shadow that he tries to run away from it. He believes that if only he could leave it behind, he would be happy. He grows increasingly distressed because, no matter how fast he runs, his shadow never once falls behind. Not about to give up, he runs faster and faster until finally he drops dead of exhaustion. It never occurred to him to stop running, to simply look over his shoulder and see that his shadow was only his body blocking the light. If he had stopped and looked back for even an instant, he would have seen the true nature of his own shadow.

This is not to suggest that your negative thoughts and feelings will vanish if you admit them to yourself. But seeing your thoughts and feelings for what they are lessens their power to scare you. What you can finally vanish is that overpowering obsession with the need to run, to hide, to cover up. You can stop running and rest in the shade of telling the truth.

Simple Truth Telling

Undefended honesty begins by telling the truth in small ways, by simply following through on doing what you say you are going to do. If you find you will not be able to do what you have said, you then tell the truth about that. Know that you will make mistakes. You may lose track of time or get distracted, but your intention can be to tell the truth in this simple way.

For example, if you say you are going to take out the trash on Sunday evening, take out the trash before you go to bed on Sunday. If you say you are going to be home at 7:00, get home by 7:00. If you find you have more work than you expected or you are stuck in traffic, call and let your partner know that circumstances have changed. Or if you suddenly look at the clock and see that you have gotten carried away with your work and will not be able to get home by 7:00, call your partner immediately and let him or her know. Apologize.

We recognize that you may feel reticent to let your partner know about a change in your plans or a lapse in awareness because of the potential initial unhappy reaction. This will be the moment to apply your growing capacities to bear uncomfortable feelings or emotions (as we discussed in Chapter 7) in relationship to your partner's reaction.

Revelatory Truth Telling

Telling the truth to another about your "shortcomings" is another form of simple truth telling that can be difficult to do. In the case of your compulsive urges, it means telling the truth about the ways you feel out of control, about the urges you have to soothe yourself with behaviors that ultimately do not serve you—the ways that you sell out on your long-term objectives for momentary relief.

In the bigger picture, it is easier to tell the truth than to lie. Yes, the impulse to protect, to lie, to fabricate, is more instinctive, but think about it. Lying requires much more calculating and strategizing in the long run. Telling the truth is simplicity at its most basic. Ultimately, it requires less energy. Even if you can only tell a small relative truth in the moment about what you are experiencing, you are closer to the seeds of your hidden unconscious motivations that are causing trouble in your life. It is not possible to hold compassion for yourself for something that you are denying even exists. For this reason alone, undefended honesty is vital to living a freer life.

Let's revisit the marshmallow experiment that we looked at in Chapter 7. A group of four- to six-year-olds was asked to resist eating a marshmallow that was sitting right in front of them. The children knew that if they could manage to resist eating that one marshmallow, they would get two marshmallows when the experimenter returned about fifteen minutes later. It turned out that the kids who could resist, those that had a higher capacity for delayed gratification, grew into adults who had more fulfilling lives.

Undefended honesty is a tool that is helpful in building your capacity for delayed gratification. Just telling the truth about what you are experiencing, especially if it is something you have the impulse to hide, takes all that energy you are using to protect yourself away from the defense mechanism and allows you to use that energy to delay gratification. When working with instinctive mechanisms, you need all the energy, attention, and internal aid you can muster.

Show Up and Tell the Truth

What else can you do while you are in the process of healing your addictive behaviors? Don't be afraid to tell your feelings and fears. Don't be afraid to confess your addictive thoughts. Don't be afraid to admit to fear, anger, and pain, even if you judge them to be the response of a child. Telling the truth leads you to authentic loving kindness. As George tells his clients, "What else can you do but tell the truth? You could buy her a diamond, but trust me, it's been done before and it doesn't work. Or at least not for very long."

William Tells the Truth

William and Betsy had been dating for about a year. William had been divorced for about ten years. His former wife finally had given up on the marriage to William because he had not been able to stop masturbating to Internet porn. The end of that marriage really got William's attention, and he had sought counseling for what he discovered were his fears of being intimate with a woman. He had begun to see how his addiction to porn was just a cover for his fears. He had come to understand that masturbating to porn was not intimate, was not connected, and he yearned for connection with a real woman. He wanted to be able to let down his defenses of perfection.

In this new relationship, he wanted to be able to connect with Betsy as the partner and equal he knew her to be. In the year they had been together, William's connection with Betsy had deepened as he slowly dissolved his fears of being run over by a woman if he allowed himself to be seen as imperfect. He had shared with her how he still had times when he felt stressed and wanted to relieve himself by going to the Internet and finding his favorite type of porn. He also told her how lucky he felt to be with a woman who was willing to share her shortcomings with him and with whom he was able to share.

One evening, William and Betsy chose to go to William's favorite Chinese restaurant. Walking inside, they were greeted by a new hostess, who was young, blonde, and a little flirty. After William and Betsy sat down and began to peruse the menus, William took a long breath and asked Betsy if he could tell her something that was hard for him to talk about. Betsy took a long breath, too, then put her menu down.

William reached across the table and took Betsy's fingertips in his hands. "I want to share something with you, but please first know how deeply committed I am to being in this relationship with you. This relationship with you is very important to me." He shared with her the attraction he had felt for the hostess as she tossed her hair when she showed them to their table. He was even able to share that the hostess had the look of the young women he used to prefer for his porn fantasies. Finally, he was able to tell Betsy that even though he had had this familiar hit of attraction, he did not want his old compulsion to get in the way of what he wanted even more—the closeness and safety he felt with Betsy.

William's words were not easy for Betsy to hear, but she felt strangely empowered by the way William had so undefendedly spoken the truth. She talked to him about what it was like for her to feel that she needed to compete for his attention. She told William that she had noticed the hostess catch his eye, and she appreciated him for "telling" on himself. She noted that his sharing of the truth actually allowed her to trust him more deeply.

William was then able to speak even more skillfully and tell Betsy that he understood how bad it must feel to be compared to other women. He admitted that he did not want to hurt her in this way. He said he was sorry. At least for that moment, he had no need to defend or protect his image.

The victory of William and Betsy's moment in the Chinese restaurant was born of William's willingness to tell the truth, to show his imperfection, as well as his willingness to risk Betsy's rejection of him because he was revealing something that he knew might cause her to feel hurt or angry with him. At the same time, Betsy was also able to openly experience and share her truth about how William's actions created feelings of inferiority for her. As a result, William and Betsy were both able to be heroes in this story.

Truth Telling Is Not a License, but a Responsibility

Telling the truth in an undefended way is a powerful tool, and, like any powerful tool, it can be misused. We are not encouraging anyone to use telling the truth as an excuse to speak in a hurtful way. Undefended truth telling should be guided by vulnerability. If you are angry, telling the truth means finding the hurt or fear underneath the anger and revealing it. In a moment of anger, it is possible that the best you can do is to say, "I'm too angry to speak right now." We are not saying there is anything wrong with feeling anger; it is an important and powerful internal signal. But with your beloved partner, you have the opportunity to ultimately undefendedly tell the truth of the fear or hurt that is hiding behind the immediate impulse of anger.

Tolerating the Imperfections

Telling the truth about your perceived imperfections is one of the steppingstones to deepening commitment and safety in your relationship. When you initially come together in a relationship, generally you create an idealized image of your partner. You overlook and smooth over the imperfections. Love seems to have a magical power of allowing you to put yourself into a trance of not noticing. As you spend more time with your partner, his or her imperfections can become painfully obvious. This is often a surprise.

After the disclosure or discovery of sexually compulsive behavior, you can deepen your relationship by allowing the disclosure of this imperfection to lead to the revelation of other imperfections. It is possible to allow this particular cascade of trouble, this tumble from whatever idealization you had of your partner, to lead to a greater capacity to tolerate imperfection in both your partner and yourself. It is possible to begin to build a team, to create a true partnership, that has the capacity to be tender with imperfection. This capacity for tenderness, for being able to tolerate the feelings stirred by imperfections (yours and your partner's), can begin to build the groundwork for greater intimacy.

In Chapter 9, we will investigate how a collision with truth can lead to an investigation of the past. Such a truthful uncovering is only possible once the idealizations have begun to crumble, once the capacity and willingness to undefendedly tell the truth has been opened.

Exercise: Making a Commitment to Each Other

At the end of Chapter 2, we asked each of you to make a commitment to yourselves. Now that you have begun to reveal yourselves to each other in a new way, now that you are beginning to build the skills of communicating with each other in an undefendedly honest way, you are ready to make a new kind of commitment to each other. This is a commitment between two individuals who have begun to strip away the masks of idealization. You may have experienced moments of being painfully imperfect. This has opened a doorway to making a commitment based on knowing more clearly what you are signing up for in your relationship.

This new commitment to each other can be whatever you as a couple now know is right for your partnership. We encourage you to word this fresh commitment as simply as possible. Write the words as a team. One of you may be the better wordsmith, but as a team, the spirit of what you hold for each other will now become apparent through the practice of undefended honesty.

When you have chosen the commitment you would like to make to each other, create a ceremony to share this promise. Buy two flowers to exchange. Set aside an evening to share a meal, to exchange the flowers, and to exchange this new and sacred promise.

CHAPTER SUMMARY

- The first person who needs your undefended honesty is you. It is not possible to hold compassion for yourself for something you are denying even exists. For this reason alone, undefended honesty is vital to living a freer life.
- Undefended, rigorous honesty is at the core of working with compulsive behavior. It is also the key to creating a foundation for rebuilding trust inside your relationship.
- Undefended honesty begins by telling the truth in small ways, by simply following through on doing what you say you are going to do.
- Telling the truth about your perceived imperfections is one of the steppingstones to deepening commitment and safety in your relationship.
- It is the journey of a hero to be willing to tell the truth undefendedly—to expose your flaws, to lay your cards on the table, to resist the impulse to defend and protect by telling a lie, or otherwise attempting to hide.

Looking Forward

In Chapter 9, we will take a tour into your past to see if there may be seeds planted in your childhood that are causing you to respond in ways that are not serving you anymore. We will share some common patterns that may help you unravel these unseen influences.

CHAPTER 9

Facing the Past: Taking a Sobering Look at How You Got Here

An issue with sexual compulsivity has caused a disruption in your relationship. If you've made it this far, the sexually compulsive partner has admitted to the problem and is working to find ways to replace the impulse for compulsive sexual behavior with the desire for intimacy and connected sex. If truth telling and willingness are here, as a couple, you now have a lot of ground to stand on. This is something to celebrate—you now have the possibility to deepen your relationship. Now is the time to explore more deeply how your past is influencing your partnership and to discover what it will take to move this relationship out of crisis mode and onto a path not only of repair but of deepening intimacy.

A relationship is a dance in which the movements of one partner influence the movements of the other. We have yet to see a troubled relationship where one person is totally the "good" party and the other is "bad." This is because both partners bring their past into the union and none of us received perfect training in how to be in a relationship.

That is why it can be helpful for each of you to question: "How did I get here?" "What is this relationship for me?" "How is my partner mirroring me and how am I mirroring my partner?"

Your Relationship Is a System

Your relationship has a life of its own. As a couple, you are both part of the system. The healing of difficulties will come at least partially through this relationship system, through the dynamics of the two of you together. As long as you both have chosen to stay in the relationship, then each partner is fully responsible for those dynamics. It's important to look at the system of the couple, and how the dynamics of the partnership are playing out in your particular challenges.

When a couple is working with an issue like sexual compulsivity, they tend to focus on "the problem," which means that the relationship dynamics might not get the attention that will ultimately help both individuals. That is why the partner with the issue of sexual compulsivity must take responsibility and make a commitment to working with the addiction.

In directing you away from focusing solely on the issue of sexual compulsivity, we're not condoning any sexual acting out. We are suggesting that, in addition to that individual attention, the couple place their focus on the dance of the relationship dynamics as well.

The Past Is Impacting the Present

How did you get to this moment? Looking to your past can provide clues. As human beings, everything we do is influenced by what we have previously learned, by the conclusions we have made about what has happened to us. Those deductions create the basic structure of our response—of how we experience the present moment. We are all more comfortable with what seems familiar than with the unfamiliar.

When you experience something new or different, you naturally attempt to classify the new experience based on what you have previously learned. You can trick yourself into thinking that something new is "just like what happened before," when it is not. That mechanism of immediate classification can cause you to overlook, misclassify, mislabel, or misinterpret a new experience by throwing it into your mind's "pile of experiences" that appear to be similar.

This does not mean you are doomed to repeat the painful experiences of your past. It is possible to bring awareness of the past into the present in a way that allows you to "rewire" or "reprogram" the past difficulties. With new awareness, the present experience that seems so reminiscent of something painful from the past can be viewed as coming back around for a "do-over."

Experiences with the Greatest Impact

As children, we depend on our caretakers. In fact, as babies, we don't even recognize that we are separate from those caretakers. We don't yet have the capacity to distinguish self from the other. As we begin to formulate a sense of self, a sense that "I exist," a sense of "me," we quite naturally identify with our caregivers. Being taken care of without having to do anything in return is a healthy part of our experience of being a baby. Brain science has determined that the internal scaffolding we create in our minds about how the world works is deeply patterned by the time we are six or seven years old.

When your experience from the past comes from a time before you had language, the impact to your view of the world can be difficult to recognize or understand. These early experiences are so familiar that they seem "normal." This doesn't mean that experiences that happen after you can understand words don't create an imprint that also deeply influences how you interpret the present moment.

However, early experiences form a view of the world in ways that ordinarily go unquestioned because they are so deeply a part of the inner landscape, your undisputed view of reality. The present moment is seen through the lens of this unquestioned internal scaffolding.

In addition to experiences that happen to the child before he or she has language, events that are more prolonged, that occur over a greater span of time, have a great influence on his or her view of how the world works. Also, any particularly traumatic event will be deeply significant. For example, physical or sexual abuse, even if it were to happen only once, would be extremely impactful.

Patterns That Affect Our View

Because these patterns of thinking, of viewing the world, have become so deeply a part of your internal landscape, it can be difficult to notice how you might be responding instinctively in ways that are not really helping you get what you want. To recognize these unseen influences, it can be helpful to learn about some basic patterns of personality put in place in the earliest years. Think of these internal influences as gremlins that are running around inside of you, causing you to respond in ways that are creating suffering and separation rather than greater connection.

Three basic patterns of survival influences that can be playing behind the scenes are issues of trust, control, and self-esteem.

- **Trust:** How safe do you feel in the world? How safe do you feel in allowing yourself to be impacted, influenced, vulnerable to another?
- **Control:** How do you prioritize your perceived needs and the needs of your partner? What are your requirements for independence and autonomy? How do you react to separation?
- **Self-Esteem:** Do you feel you matter in the world? Do you feel you have a right to exist?

As a child, given the best information and support that you had at the time, you came to conclusions about trust, control, and self-esteem. Allow yourself to look at the patterns of suffering in your life and relationship. Allow the observer within you to see how you are being impacted in the present by the scaffolding of conclusions or assumptions that you made in response to classifications that may have been faulty conclusions.

The Roots of the Past Are Woven Into the Present

The origins of many behaviors that show up in the present, including sexually compulsive behaviors, can be found in the past. You might visualize the present as being like a large oak tree in the front yard of an old house. The roots of the tree are not seen, but they are there, buried beneath ground level. In fact, the roots can grow underneath the sidewalk leading to the front door, causing the sidewalk to buckle. This affects anyone walking on it now, in the present. Or a root can grow into a drainage pipe, obstructing the flow and causing a bathtub to not drain properly. The point is that these unseen "roots" representing the past impact what is happening now. In that sense, they are not "just" the past; they are also living as part of the present. They are both.

This is the case with sexually compulsive behavior. For the man who has a pattern of sexually compulsive behavior, it's time to both accept how he is behaving in the present and search for the specific roots of this behavior in the past. By first stopping the sexually compulsive behavior and then exploring the roots of that behavior, he can ensure those roots no longer have the same unseen impact.

If a boy grows up in a family where the father was focused on money and saw the wife and mother as a means for sexual pleasure and home-cooked meals, that boy will not have a model for healthy intimacy. Instead, as an adult, that man might seek virtual "relationships" with women on porn sites. Such relationships are, in fact, a version of what he knows from childhood where his father also had essentially virtual, rather than real, relationships. This is the past having a strong impact on the present (or the past and present overlapping as one).

Correspondingly, the wife may have grown up in a family where the father was more interested in his work than in having a close, intimate, relationship with his wife. The little girl also learns from her family, and her past impacts her present when she chooses a man. She will most likely not make this choice consciously. Yet unconsciously, she may have been drawn to a man who does not seek intimacy. She may not be happy with the choice, but like the man she chose, she, too, is entangled in the roots of the past and has yet to break free. Although she may not act out sexually, her past has impacted her present through her choices.

As children, we yearn to behave in a way that will make our parents love us. If our parents are uncomfortable, they push us away and shame us with their stern looks or reproachful words. Thus, we learn to behave in ways that do not make our parents ill at ease. To adapt ourselves to the needs of our parents, we may hide our true feelings and learn to repress and avoid. As we grow more distant from our own true feelings, we are no longer able to connect with others from a place of what we truly feel. We are entangled in the roots of the past, which strongly influence our actions in the present.

Similar to how he felt shamed in childhood, a man who is now married may again feel shame for his sexually compulsive behavior. He may feel this shame both from himself and from his spouse. In effect, he is repeating the past. One way to stop repeating the past is to uncover and acknowledge your feelings from the past, and embrace whatever has happened to you in the past along with what is happening now. This is how you can be truly aware of your feelings and thoughts as well as your impulses to sexually act out, to feel shame, and to shame others.

By following the directives of the previous chapter on undefended honesty, a man can begin to disentangle the roots of the past he is reacting to with his sexually compulsive behavior. Next, as he disentangles himself from the stranglehold of the roots of the past, he can allow his healthy impulses to emerge, impulses such as the desire for true connection and intimacy with a real person.

Steven and Emily

Steven and Emily came to us after they had been married for twenty years. Emily had inadvertently discovered evidence on Steven's computer of his activities with prostitution and other kinds of meetings for sex. She knew that she hadn't felt connected with Steven for a long time, and this was the final straw for her. She reported that Steven had seemed totally consumed with his trips around the country to play golf. Since their three boys were now grown and had left home, she felt that she had tried every way she knew to get her husband's attention, to interest him in their marriage and partnership again, to allow her to be a part of his life.

Steven admitted that he had gotten involved in looking for companionship online. He was embarrassed that he had allowed himself to get caught in what he felt was a pretty seamy world of what he labeled "casual hook-ups." He couldn't really understand why he had felt so compelled to keep going back to these sites. He admitted that he really wanted to make his relationship with Emily work, but that he didn't know how. He could see that he was somehow pushing his wife away. He was able to admit that the golf with his buddies and the Internet dating seemed to require so much less effort than trying to please Emily. He said he felt like she had left him long ago. They both felt they had been abandoned by the other. Steven had acted out sexually and needed to admit that and atone for those actions. They both needed to see how the seeds of their past were playing out in the present.

Steven and Emily's Past

Steven and Emily had been high school sweethearts. They grew up in a small town, and went away to college together. Steven studied business and Emily studied to become an elementary school teacher. They both always knew that they wanted to get married and have a family together. So when they graduated from college and Steven got a great entry-level position at an investment bank, they felt they were on their way to living out their destiny.

But they each had experiences from their growing-up years, some scaffolding of their view of relationships that had been put into place in their earliest years, that came back to haunt them as their relationship matured. As much as they loved each other, as much as they held a shared vision of being together, these unseen influences were waiting for them.

Steven's father had walked out when Steven was three. Steven never really knew the whole story about what had happened. As he looked back on it after he was grown, he suspected that maybe his mother had been having an affair with a neighbor. His mother always told the story that his father "went out for a pack of cigarettes and never came back."

When Steven was five, his mother married a man who was a long-distance truck driver. Steven felt close to his new father figure. He liked him. But Steven remembers how his mother would frequently wonder aloud when his stepfather went out on the road whether or not he would come back. His mother would say, "He could always turn out to be just like your father," and she would retell the story of the trip for cigarettes that ended in abandonment.

Whenever Steven's stepfather was away, Steven's mother would tell him how he was now the "man of the house." Steven remembers how his mother would have male friends in to spend the night when his stepfather was away. His mother told him he could never tell his stepfather about these visitors. As her man of the house, he was in charge of guarding her secret.

Emily brought her own history to the relationship. Her father ran an insurance agency and her mother was a high school teacher. Emily's father was a quiet, unassuming kind of guy. Her mother ran the household—she was gregarious, outgoing, and liked to be involved in every aspect of Emily's life.

From as early as she could remember, Emily reported that she felt like her mother never "left her alone." Emily said that she always had the feeling that her mother had to know everything about her. She had memories from her early teens of her mother standing in the next room to listen in on her phone calls. Since her mother was one of the teachers at the school where Emily went to high school, she felt that there was no escape from her mother's ever-present oversight. Emily responded by being a perfect daughter and a perfect student. She was even the valedictorian of her graduating class. Since she felt like she was being monitored all the time, she chose to be as good as possible. By being perfect, her mother wouldn't have anything to worry about and Emily could feel safe.

The Past Is Affecting Your Relationship

Neither partner has come to this relationship as a blank slate. You bring everything you have learned about love and relationship both consciously and unconsciously with you into the relationship. We all bring the past to life in our present relationships. We can't help it.

Ordinarily, your first relationship was with your parents. Your mother was probably your primary caregiver during your most formative years. The nature of that relationship has been shown to set the template for your unconscious expectations, especially in your closest, most intimate relationship. You are quite likely unaware of the ways that past influences can invade your intimate partnership. Present experiences appear as a version of the past returning so that you can redeem or rework the unfinished business. You return to what is familiar precisely because it is known rather than unknown. Even an uncomfortable known interpretation feels more "natural" than an interpretation that is unknown, potentially threatening, and thus scary.

Your intimate relationship brings these past influences into the present in a way that, try as you might, you cannot ignore. When you re-experience a desirable quality of relationship from the past, your current relationship is enhanced. However, when your past (and early) unfilled needs for trust, control, or self-esteem are activated by a current situation, you have the opportunity to recognize the experience for what it is—and then learn from it. That allows you to reclaim and rework these past difficulties. The container of relationship allows you to bring new awareness to situations that seem to be a replay of something from the past. The information and feedback that is available in undefended truth telling with your intimate partner brings with it the capacity to reveal your blind spots, the conclusions from your past that you cannot recognize are acting as your filter of how you view the world.

Steven and Emily's Marriage

During the first years of Emily and Steven's marriage, the focus was on their growing family and their three little boys. Steven devoted much of his time to earning a good living, while Emily was dedicated to being a good mother. Emily felt that Steven was not as connected to her as he used to be. He seemed so focused on becoming successful that he didn't seem to notice the times that Emily tried to get his attention, made a special dinner, or attempted to engage him sexually.

Both Steven and Emily later recalled moments during these first five years of their marriage when they wanted to talk, but the other seemed preoccupied with either job or family. Steven recalled a moment of rushing home to tell Emily he had landed a big new account, but when he got home that day all three boys as well as Emily had bad colds, and Emily was not available to listen to him.

Emily had her own memories of Steven's unavailability. She recalled cooking special birthday meals for Steven on nights when he ended up not coming home until very late. He had been so focused on his work at the office that he had forgotten the birthday meal. Each of them could recall moments big and small when they had experienced disappointment and disconnection. Both had given up on reaching out to the other for companionship.

The moment of Emily's discovery of Steven's online activities was a moment of collision for their marriage. Emily was ready to leave the marriage, but they both felt the pull of that original connection to each other. They felt there was something here to save.

This required Emily and Steven to each be 100 percent responsible for the success or failure of the marriage.

The first step was for Steven to commit to ceasing any sort of sexual activity outside of the marriage. He was deeply aware that those ventures lacked intimate connection. Using terminology from the financial field in which he worked, he told us how his investment in that type of activity did not have the payoff he ultimately desired.

Steven and Emily both agreed to look at their unseen past influences to see what might be driving their feelings of distance and protection. Steven was able to understand his desire to protect himself from the hurt he felt whenever he reached out to Emily and she responded in a way that he thought was angry or disapproving. His dislike of feeling rejected by Emily caused him to be constantly on guard, and his first impulse was to blame Emily for "making him feel rejected."

Then Steven was able to remember how he had that same feeling as a boy when his stepfather would go away and his mother would speculate that he might not come back. He could remember deciding as a young boy to never allow anyone to abandon him. He concluded that he could take care of himself by meeting his own needs. His mother's example of looking for men outside of the marriage had become Steven's model of how to act inside of a marriage. He saw that now, as an adult, he had the opportunity to make a different choice.

When Emily reached back into her past, she clearly saw how she felt she needed to protect herself from her mother's invasiveness. She began to see how angry she had felt about it and how she still had that anger. She saw how she had chosen to make herself "good" rather than have to experience what she thought was bad—being angry with her mother. She began to see how she had felt angry with Steven for what she perceived as his abandonment of her. Rather than openly expressing her anger with Steven, however, she had gotten busy doing what she knew how to do. She became good. She became the best mother she could be, focusing her attention on making sure her children were cared for while withholding her attention (and anger) from Steven.

She began to understand how she had walled herself off from Steven. With this knowledge, she then recognized that in her relationship with her husband, she no longer needed to repeat the past by recreating the wall she had built to protect herself from her mother. She really did not want to keep Steven away.

Emily had to clearly experience and speak with Steven about her anger. And Steven had to listen to Emily's anger and tell her how he understood why she was angry with him. Steven's willingness to hear her anger, and his sincere regret at having hurt her, created a new experience for Emily. She was able to see how she did not have to be "good" to be loved. Steven began to see that he was not being abandoned by Emily. Even if Emily was unhappy with him, he did not have to relive the abandonment of his father walking out. As a result of their realizations about the past and making new choices in the present, Emily and Steven's behavior was forever changed.

The Transformative Power of Relationship

If and when you and your partner can gain even a small amount of perspective about how the past is impacting your present, this awareness has the potential to transform and enhance your relationship. If you simply replay your past without recognizing and understanding it, your relationship will be troubled. Even a small amount of willingness to uncover and look at the beliefs and images, the scaffolding that you have brought to your union, can lead to worthwhile results. The power of your connection, the desire that you feel to be with your partner, can act as a carrot to a horse, leading you to investigate areas that you would otherwise internally label "do not disturb."

When you allow your partner to really matter to you, you allow new experiences to help you rebuild your relationship scaffolding. You can create a new view. With this view, you can look to the ways you have come together with your partner so you can rework the past.

I'm Not Getting My Needs Met

At times, one partner or the other can become focused on "my needs." If you are demanding that your partner meet your needs, you are possibly overlooking your responsibility to the relationship itself. The relationship needs to be a container that allows the past to live in the present in a way that encourages the reworking of your negative (and probably unseen) views of how relationships work. If either party remains solely focused on their individual needs, the relationship will stall. The needs of the relationship, as well as the frailties of each partner, need to be held tenderly and put on an equal footing with the needs of the individual.

Being in a relationship requires a balance of placing value and priority on your individual desire for feeling safe, being in control, and experiencing value (self-esteem), while at the same time placing value on providing safety, yielding control, and supporting the self-esteem of your partner. To the extent that you do not have healthy internal structures in one or more of these areas, you may experience the impulse to demand repayment from your partner for internal structures not properly created when you were very young. But your partner cannot rebuild these structures for you.

You can, however, give and receive support in finding the internal strength, courage, and compassion to face what can feel like overwhelming impulses. Some of these may be:

- You may experience an uncomfortable sense that if your partner gets what he or she wants, then you will not get what you want.
- It may be tempting to make your partner wrong, so you can feel right.
- It can be difficult to allow your beloved to just be as he or she is or to allow the situation to just be as it is.
- It can be difficult to allow your partner's view of reality to be as true as your view of reality.

But it is possible to permit seemingly contradictory viewpoints to both be "correct." The solution, the way out of a perceived impasse, can come from broadening your perspective to include what seems to be the opposite point of view. As strange as it may sound, you and your partner can both be right; you just have different viewpoints based on the particular perspective of your past influences.

How the Relationship Can Support You

Each partner in the relationship needs to feel honored in a way that he or she feels safe. To get a picture of this primary need for safety, imagine a two-year-old child who is venturing away from mother, and in the next instant turning back for reassurance that mother is still there. In the same way, in our most intimate relationships, we have the need to feel accepted while we also express our individuality. To the extent that your structures of safety, dominion, and self-esteem were not adequately put in place when you were young, you will need to rebuild them now. A relationship is quite often the arena where the absence of these structures becomes uncomfortably obvious. Your partner cannot prevent you from having an experience of vulnerability. Particularly in intimate relationships, all of us can experience a terrifying sense of vulnerability that we try to hide from ourselves, and certainly from anyone else.

In our most intimate relationships, we unknowingly allow our partner to "step into the shoes," both positively and negatively, of the people, such as parents, who helped formulate our original structures of self-esteem. To the extent that our parents were wounded, incapable, damaged, or just too young, they were not capable of allowing us to safely attach in a way that we could build functional structures of safety, dominion, and self-esteem. This is not an excuse to blame your parents for their shortcomings; undoubtedly, their early life experience taught them how to parent.

When you can see how the past is impacting your present, you have a chance to rebuild your structures of trust, control, and self-esteem. Your intimate relationship is the place you can rebuild, cooperatively, as loving witnesses to each other.

When either partner's past wounding comes to visit, if both partners can find ways to be especially tender and attentive, healing can occur. This is not to keep the wounded state in place or to coddle it. The intention is to cooperate tenderly with each other, not to meet the unmet needs, but to help each other find internal tenderness.

Generally, we all desire freedom. In intimate relationships, our wounded places can scream out to be met. Willingness from both partners in the relationship can create a tender space for re-examination of early conclusions that have created faulty structures of trust, control, and self-esteem. What is needed is not getting your way or "being right," but internally allowing the uncomfortable experience of your perceived need to be met with loving kindness and awareness.

A Cautionary Note

Both partners must agree not to use what they have learned of the other's past as a way to make a point or "win" an argument. Even when you can clearly see an underlying pattern in your beloved, it is not your place to become the therapist. An example of the way you would not want to talk with your partner is, "Clearly you are seeing me as your mother. If you could just see this pattern as clearly as I can see it, then you would stop treating me so badly." Without an agreement to refrain from "helping" in this way, each of you will not be able to create the container of safety necessary to venture into the territory of the past with your partner.

In working with wounds from the past, it is important to tread gently and respectfully, with yourself and with your partner. This is not an area to use the force of your will, your sense of knowledge, or any sense of superiority. Neither partner gets to be more "expert" in the relationship. You are finding your way with each other through uncharted territory. By tenderly honoring your partner's needs, you can help create a ledge of safety from the abyss of past wounds. Judgment, being right, or seeing your partner's faults and pointing them out does not foster respect and does not create a ground of safety. Sometimes wounds from the past are so tender they need to be protected from the slightest breeze of harsh judgment. Caring and compassion can coax even the most wounded parts of ourselves out of the deep dark cave in which they may have taken refuge.

Steven and Emily's Discoveries

Individually, as Steven and Emily began to take 100 percent responsibility for the dynamics of their relationship, they began to be able to soften to the other. The first big breakthrough came when Emily suggested that she accompany Steven on one of his golfing trips. In the past, she had not wanted to go on these trips. She felt left out when Steven went to play golf, but she decided she would go along and enjoy herself by sitting by the pool and doing something she loved to do—read. Because the golf courses were located at lovely resorts, she could even treat herself with a massage.

In the evenings, they went for quiet dinners together. One night, Steven began to talk with Emily about their mutual investments. She felt included. In return, Steven began to feel her acceptance of his special skills in being able to make and manage money. They both began to understand how they had been able to bring the past into the present in a way that healed old patterns and replaced them with care and kindness for each other.

You Can Limit the Scope of Your Investigation

If your view of the present is being obscured by past assumptions or scaffolding from your history, it will leave clues that you can recognize. This is another helpful time to think like a detective, to round up your clues. Look for patterns. Pay particular attention if you find that more than one person has a similar suggestion, complaint, or piece of advice for you. Notice if you are having an experience that feels like a repeating pattern. Check to see if, over and over again, your life seems to be a story with a vaguely familiar plotline or ending.

It may help to imagine that your clear experience of the present moment is like standing in a beautiful field. If you somehow find yourself in a dense forest, with the trees being the influences from your past that are blocking your clear view, you still know the sunny meadow is out there somewhere. However, the only way to reach the clarity of the beautiful field is to travel through the forest. The only way out of the forest is through it.

This doesn't mean you need to stop and investigate every tree in the forest. Your investigation of the past does not need to be a major research project. You don't need to uncover your entire past or every incident that may be impacting you today. You don't need to move boulders, when all that is required is to move a couple of stones. If you have a leak in your bathroom, you don't need to tear up your entire house.

In looking to the past, start with the present. What in the present is creating difficulty? From that point of entry, you can begin to ask yourself how you may be making assumptions and conclusions in the present that keep you reacting in the same old ways, rather than creating a fresh moment for you and your partner.

Exercise: Blazing a Trail Into the Past

To discover the most pertinent influences from your past, the best place to start is with whatever is troubling you in the present moment. In particular, bring to mind the thing about your partner that is the most troubling to you. As an example, "I feel like my husband/wife is not willing to take responsibility."

Now take that particular problem or issue and turn it around. Make yourself the problem; make the complaint about you. We recognize this will probably seem like the last thing you would want to do, but you won't have to tell your partner or anyone else how you have tried to explore this issue by turning the complaint back around to you.

As difficult as it may seem, this technique is invaluable in revealing a view of the world that you might not be able to see in any other way. As unlikely as it may seem to you, much of the time, a complaint you have about your partner is in some way similar to a complaint your partner has about you.

In the example above, you might attempt to turn this complaint around in a couple of ways. You might contemplate (as impossible as it may initially seem) a thought like, "I do not want to take responsibility for something I have done." You also might find that the reflected feeling on the other side of this complaint might be something like, "I haven't been able to see how I feel responsible for something my father/mother did to me." Or perhaps, "I haven't been able to see how I feel responsible for how my father/mother felt about me."

What we have seen, again and again, is that a shortcoming you perceive in your partner that continues to irritate you is generally a clue that an assumption from the past is affecting some part of your view of the present. Let's take another example. Say your complaint with your partner is, "My partner does not meet my needs." To flip that around for further investigation, you might ask yourself, "How do I not meet my partner's needs?" Or you may ask yourself, "How am I not willing to pay attention to or provide for my own needs?" Again, we recognize that it will not feel natural to look at the opposite side or the flip of your complaint. It is much more natural to want to stick with your ordinary view about this complaint about your partner. But because this is an investigation designed to reveal how the past is playing in the present, it will be extremely helpful for you to put aside your natural defenses.

Let this grievance in the present lead you into your past. Does this thought, this way of thinking remind you in any way of something familiar? How does this remind you of how you felt when you were small? If an answer does not immediately come to mind, don't force a conclusion. Allow yourself to come back to this investigation as many times as you feel may be necessary to allow your native intelligence to provide the information that will help you see what you need to see.

Finally, whether or not you have found some clue to the past, take your complaint about your partner, as well as its reverse, and just for this moment allow all of these hurts and complaints to dissolve into nothing. Give yourself and your partner just a momentary reprieve. Let all those hurts and accusations turn into smoke and be blown away with the wind. Anything that needs to return will come back when required. We promise, you will not need to go looking.

CHAPTER SUMMARY

- Your past is impacting your present. When you experience something new or different, you naturally attempt to classify the new experience based on what you have previously learned.
- The origins of many behaviors that show up in the present, including sexually compulsive behaviors, can be found in the past. In the same way, you bring everything you have learned about love and relationship both consciously and unconsciously with you into your relationship.
- A relationship is a dance in which the movements of one partner influence the movements of the other. As a couple, you are both part of the system. The healing of difficulties will come at least partially through this relationship system, through the dynamics of the two of you together.

- When you can see how the past is impacting your present, you have a chance to rebuild your structures of trust, control, and self-esteem. Your intimate relationship is the place you can rebuild, cooperatively, as loving witnesses to each other.
- One way to stop repeating the past is to uncover, acknowledge, and embrace whatever has happened in the past as well as what is happening now. This is how you can be truly aware of your feelings and thoughts as well as your impulses to sexually act out, feel shame, and shame others.

Looking Forward

Now that you have begun to take the necessary steps to rebuild your relationship, we begin Part 3, "Moving Forward," with a look at strengthening your intimate connection. In the next chapter, we explore building sexual intimacy by developing skills of intimate communication.

PART THREE

MOVING FORWARD

CHAPTER 10

Building Intimacy

The desire for intimacy is a basic human longing. We yearn to belong, to love, to be connected with another. It's no accident that songs, films, and photos depict stories of love. We are all pulled toward that amazing connection with another human being. And intimacy can be a truly joyful experience beyond anything typically depicted on the screen.

However, in the media that influences us, there has been a blurring of love with sex, and intimacy has been used euphemistically to speak about sexual contact. In this chapter, we are talking about intimacy more fully—as the capacity to reveal ourselves, as the willingness and desire to be completely real with another. The point is that the experience of real intimacy is better than anything you could have ever imagined.

Revealing our hidden inner influences, being real and undefended, can be tricky because we can only be as true with another as we are undefended with ourselves. In addition, to the extent that we allow ourselves to be impacted by our partner, to be more fully aware of our inner workings, we allow ourselves an ever-deepening experience of intimacy. It is a cycle that builds on itself. The willingness to be exposed, to see, builds even greater intimacy both for our own inner workings and with our beloved.

Collusion, Collision, and Collaboration

The vast majority of relationships never attain true intimacy. For many people, the unhappiness they feel about their relationship is similar to having a small pain in the ankle that is not really hurting enough to do something about. Instead, they live with it. However, if the ankle was broken and the pain was excruciating, they would need to address it. Because your relationship has been "broken," and you are addressing it, you have the wonderful opportunity to rebuild it in a new way, to attain true intimacy.

The collision caused by the revelation of the sexually compulsive behavior has the capacity to lead to a deeper level of collaboration, which can lead to greater intimacy. Each partner will participate in one way or another in the ultimate outcome of the life of your partnership. Moving into deeper cooperation with your partner requires that both of you take full responsibility for yourselves and for the relationship. In a codependent relationship, one or both partners collude by keeping their focus on changing the other rather than on changing themselves and thus changing the nature of the relationship itself.

If your partner is not showing up to take responsibility or to engage with you, you cannot use coercion, or begging, or crying. To attempt to force the collaboration of your partner when he or she is unable to take the step into the realm of collaboration is not a path that will lead to greater intimacy. Greater intimacy requires the willingness of both partners to move into areas that have up to now been hidden.

Collaboration requires commitment from both partners. Although each partner may, from time to time, waver in their desire to remain in the relationship, in order to move past the impasse of a difficult time, both partners need to remain committed to full participation. Although there can be unbearable pain in the process of deepening intimacy, this crisis is transforming both you and your relationship.

Merging and Independence

At times, each partner must leap into new and unknown territory of yielding to the other. Both surrendering control and taking full responsibility are required. It may seem like a paradox, but the two qualities work hand in hand. Intimacy is built through the capacity to maintain a sense of yourself while at the same time being able to have compassion in an undefended way for your partner's needs and wants. The capacity to reveal the parts of yourself that feel the most ugly, weak, or vulnerable requires inner strength.

Part of the inner sturdiness required is knowing that you are going to be disappointed by your partner and that you can bear the disappointment. Intimacy can be built even in those times of disappointment—if you are able to fully express your hurt and your partner is able to show empathy for your experience.

If your sense of independence is overly threatened by getting close to your partner, then intimacy will suffer. For example, one client reported that he felt that he was "doing as he was told" (and that seemed dangerous) when he experienced that his wife was asking too much of him. He felt like a powerless child who was in danger. In these moments, he would become angry and push his wife's needs and requests away because his own sense of individual identity or autonomy felt threatened. As he was able to strengthen his own inner sense of satisfaction, safety, and peace in the world, he found he did not need to crumble when he sensed he was disappointing his wife.

The deepening of love and intimacy requires the willingness to make the needs and wants of the other, and of the relationship, just as important as your individual needs and wants. The capacity of surrendering self to other brings with it the benefit of intimacy. We bask in those unguarded moments of sinking into intimacy. We all want to merge, yet we fear merging.

It can be helpful to visualize yourself and your partner as two stable buildings standing side by side, firmly planted in the ground. If one of the structures becomes shaky or destabilized in some way, but the other is still standing firm, it can even prop up the wavering structure temporarily until stability can be re-established. If, however, the two structures have been set up to remain standing by leaning on each other (resting on the ground at the base, but propped against each other at the top), and one structure goes down, then they both go down. Intimacy is enhanced when you know you are firmly supported internally (an inner sense of independence and strength) and you can remain open and supportive to your partner. A sense of independence (I can take care of myself) and a capacity to merge (I can allow myself to feel helpless) are both required for intimacy to bloom.

The Vital Reflection from Your Partner

When you are willing and able to allow yourself to become undefended with your partner, it becomes more likely that you will experience moments of intimacy. It may come as a surprise that divulging what can seem to be your worst and weakest qualities to your partner creates intimacy. Revealing yourself to your partner, and allowing yourself to be impacted by his or her revelations to you, can help uncover the thought patterns, perceptions, and conclusions that you hold about the world that are actually self-defeating. Your normal way of looking at the world is incorporated so unconsciously into ordinary perceptions and conclusions that defenses can remain invisible and hidden. The viewpoint of your partner can help you see more clearly into your individual style of self-protection—a protection that actually keeps you away from intimacy.

The way you perceive your relationship, the way you see your partner, or hear what they have said, is colored by the way you view the world. We described this view of the world in the previous chapter as scaffolding. These perceptions are your filters. These filters can cause your interpreted view of the world, your projections—which could, in reality, be false—to be experienced as perceptions that you believe to be true. The process of becoming intimate with your partner, of allowing yourselves to intimately view the world and yourself through the eyes of your partner, can reveal unseen defenses. When you stretch your immediate view of the world to include your partner's viewpoint, you are less likely to be blindsided by your unseen assumptions and conclusions, and you bring down your barriers of safety that prevent the experience of intimacy.

Building Safety Through Intimate Communication

Developing deeper intimacy in your relationship requires a sincere sense of safety. When trust has been broken, safety has been shattered. The collision of this crisis has certainly disrupted the experience of safety in your relationship. As trust is rebuilt, safety can also be rebuilt and can deepen. That quality of safety is generated partly internally, by trusting that you can bear any tsunami of your own strong feelings and emotions, and partly by the experience of baring yourself to your partner and being held in that nakedness. It is not a coincidence that we use the words bare and naked here when discussing emotional intimacy: Emotional intimacy fosters sexual intimacy.

Emotional intimacy requires that you put down your defenses. In previous chapters, we've looked at developing your capacity for greater vulnerability by working with tendencies toward blame and shame, by sorting out your strong feelings, by building your capacity for undefended honesty, and by looking at how you are being influenced in the present by your past. Now you are being called to bring all those elements into play so you can communicate in a more intimate way. Intimate conversation is built on two skills: reflecting and expressing compassionate understanding.

Reflecting

Reflecting is mirroring. As you know, the best mirror is smooth, clear, and free of distortion. It can be a tall order to be a clear mirror to your intimate partner, to simply repeat or reflect back without distortion exactly what is being said to you—especially when what your partner has to say creates an uncomfortable emotional response in you. As we mentioned earlier, your capacity to stay separate from your partner, to maintain your own inner integrity, is like being a fully rooted structure on the ground. This inner strength will allow you to let your partner's experience remain your partner's experience, and not become tangled up with your reaction. You need to be able to keep yourself safe from your partner's feelings, to put aside your own emotional response, so you can really listen to and hear your partner's feelings.

Reflecting is simply putting what your partner has said to you in your own words. It can also include asking your partner to explain further. The goal of great reflecting is to help your partner more fully understand what he or she is thinking and feeling. Your part in the investigation is to help your partner be a better detective about what is going on internally. Be interested. Reflect and compassionately understand. You do not have to agree or disagree. This is not the moment for a debate, a weighing of options, or an analysis of the merits of your partner's conclusions.

It is important to not push or force. That can create defensiveness in your partner. The experience of really being heard by another person who is not trying to change you or defend against what you are saying creates a sense of safety and intimacy.

Reflecting skillfully can be difficult because it requires the partner who is doing the reflecting to—at least for a few moments—put aside his or her own personal defenses and reactions. Don't expect to be able to reflect without reacting every time your partner speaks to you. Sometimes you will react internally, and can't put the reaction on pause. In those instances, please remember to forgive yourself and gently admit the truth of your reaction.

Compassionate Understanding

The second step of intimate conversation, expressing compassionate understanding, builds on the skill of reflecting. Compassionate understanding does not require agreement with your partner; it simply requires awareness and comprehension. Try to understand what your partner is experiencing. Try to see the world through his or her eyes just for this moment and see how, from his or her point of view, what is being expressed might make sense.

For your partner to receive the fullness of your empathy, your understanding needs to be communicated in words. Express whatever understanding you can find about your partner's experience, not to change it, fix it, or correct it, but simply to acknowledge that it exists. "I can see why you felt so hurt when I withdrew from you. I understand how that must have felt like I had abandoned you." Note that the key to these words is, "I understand why you feel that way." This is also a good moment to say, "I'm sorry."

An intimate conversation involves give and take. As each of you finds that you are building your skills of reflecting and expressing compassionate understanding, you will discover that the safety needed for intimacy will naturally begin to flower.

Josh and Lisa

In Chapter 3, you met Josh and Lisa, who had been able to take concrete steps toward a more intimate relationship after Lisa discovered Josh's secret life and compulsion with online porn. After the initial discovery, explosion, revelation, open sharing, and then the closeness he had felt with Lisa in those first few weeks, Josh felt that she had begun to grow somewhat cold and distant. She had been a bit sharp when he asked her questions. At night, she hadn't been snuggling up to him as they slept. She was sleeping on her own side of the bed.

He felt those old familiar yearnings to go online. He was able to tell himself that he knew he wanted intimacy with Lisa more than he wanted the porn, but he also realized that he didn't really know what to do next. So he asked her to go out to dinner with him. The following conversation that unfolded at that dinner was one of the steps Josh and Lisa took toward establishing greater intimacy in their relationship.

Josh waited to talk about what was on his mind until after they had finished eating and had ordered their after-dinner coffee. Although he felt tentative about telling Lisa what he was feeling, he decided to take the risk. He knew he could only start with what he knew in the moment, even though it might upset Lisa.

Josh also knew the alternative was that he was going to go back online and, if he did that, the consequences to his marriage would be severe. He had begun to recognize that the porn was a dead end. He was afraid that Lisa would think he was not a man if he shared with her how weak he felt. But he remembered how she had accepted the facts of his past—facts that he had previously been sure no one would ever accept.

He decided to be totally honest. "Lisa, I've been really wanting to go online for the last few days. I feel like maybe you are still mad at me about the porn—or maybe it's something else. I can't tell. I'd like to understand what's going on."

For a moment, Lisa felt a pang of anger. He was talking about the thing she was the most afraid of—that he would just keep going back to the porn. But here he was, talking to her about it. Then she thought, perhaps this might be a good sign. And since he'd asked the question, she had to stop herself for a moment to see if she might be angry. She realized that she was indeed feeling angry about the porn. She had been feeling angry that she had married someone who was attracted to porn. She hadn't wanted to talk to Josh about it, because she was afraid it would hurt him or push him back online. Now she realized that since she wanted intimacy, it was important that she find some way to speak to Josh about this thing that was troubling her so much.

She remembered the analogy of what an intimate partnership is—not leaning on each other but still available to each other. She stopped just for a moment to feel her inner sense of strength. "Yes, I have been feeling angry. You're right. I am angry that this problem is a part of our marriage. I don't like it."

Then she paused and realized there was more. "Really, I'm afraid that you will go back to the porn and I will have to go through the pain again that I felt in that moment of opening the spare bedroom door and seeing you in front of those awful images."

Josh thought about the skill of reflecting. His first impulse was to defend himself, to let Lisa know how wrong she was, but he stopped himself, took a deep breath, and spoke with a skill that surprised him. He was able to reflect Lisa's words back to her. "You're angry that I was using porn, and you don't like it. You're afraid that I won't be able to control myself, that I'll just keep doing it and you'll get hurt all over again."

Josh's reflection was so undefended that Lisa smiled. "Yes," she said, "that is exactly what I'm feeling. Thank you."

Josh, with the success of his reflecting, decided he might as well practice compassionate understanding as well. He told us later that when we had first explained these skills to them, he had thought this was something only a saint could do, not a regular guy like him. But we had assured him that it was possible. He had been thinking about how hard it would have been for him if the tables had been turned, and he had discovered Lisa looking at online porn. So that night in the restaurant, rather than defending himself, he decided he would share this understanding with Lisa.

"I can understand how you would feel hurt about what I was doing while I was looking at all those other women online. I can see why that hurt you. And I can understand why you would be afraid that I'd do it again. It makes perfect sense to me that you would feel that way. I'm sorry."

Just for this moment, he stopped himself from explaining to her about all the effort he had put into converting his urges to go online into something more productive, and about how proud he felt about how he was learning to work with himself. He would save that for a conversation they would have later during which Lisa would reflect his words and offer her compassionate understanding about his struggle with porn and how aware she was of the changes he was making.

That night when they went home, the depth of the emotional intimacy of their conversation, the safety created by sharing and being heard and accepted, opened the doorway to physical intimacy. As they contentedly drifted off into dreamland, Lisa did not sleep on her side of the bed.

Intimate Sexuality

The experience of intimate, connected sex is based on a connection born of vulnerability, trust (built through honesty), and compassionate connection. Intimate, loving sex and compulsive or addictive sex are not the same thing. Engaging in compulsive or addictive sex is not a steppingstone toward intimate, connected sex. You have directly experienced how damaging compulsive sexual behaviors can be to the intimacy you would like to have in your relationship.

When the natural sexual connection you have with your partner is combined with your vulnerable loving connection, it becomes possible for each of you to surrender into giving and receiving the natural pleasure of your bodies. The pleasure and playfulness of connecting sexually inside of your committed relationship can promote the development of a sexual history with your partner that is unique to you as a couple. You both get to make it up as you go. Your bodies and the connection between your two bodies will be your guide.

Compulsive addictive sex can be thought of as simply remaining focused on the sex act itself. Intimate sex brings love, connection, compassion, and intimacy into the picture, that's why it is called making love. Intimate sex takes your sexual energies and weds them with the forces of empathy, identification, and oneness that you experience in intimately surrendering with your partner. The dance of pleasing your partner and being pleased by your partner deepens as you are able to let go into the safety you experience in intimately revealing yourselves to each other. As your hearts open, the walls come down, and your bodies can respond like an uninhibited, passionate dancer responding to his or her favorite music. In the intimacy of meeting your partner in this way, sexual passion can actually continue to become more fulfilling over time as you mature your intimate connection with your partner.

Forgiveness

In Chapter 5, we discussed the re-establishing of trust as a means to forgiveness. As you build the capacities we have discussed in the preceding chapters, intimacy will be fostered and forgiveness will more gracefully begin to be established. More forgiveness brings more intimacy. Forgiveness in many ways is a byproduct of building intimacy. You have the capacity to block forgiveness or to foster it.

Forgiveness is promoted by many of the same skills that support intimacy. The more you can see the world through your partner's eyes, the more deeply you will be able to bring forgiveness to what has happened. These are not experiences you need to rush yourself into having. All of your anger, grief, frustration, and hurt can still be honored while you intimately explore the world as viewed by your beloved.

You have probably heard that if you are seeking forgiveness, first forgive. Forgiveness begins with forgiving yourself. As you build compassion and empathy for yourself, you will be able to build compassion and empathy for your partner. The wisdom from the beautiful prayer attributed to the thirteenth century Saint Francis of Assisi applies here—it is true that "in giving we receive."

Monitoring Your Partner

In Chapter 2, we discussed the monitoring of e-mail accounts, computer access, cell phone calls, or other portals that your partner may have used to indulge his sexual compulsivity. Initially, it may create a greater feeling of safety for both partners to use a shared e-mail account, monitoring devices, monitoring software, or blocking software, but in the long run, in order to develop trust and intimacy, the partner with the sexual compulsivity issue must take responsibility for himself. Monitoring or being monitored does not foster intimacy. It is difficult for the partner doing the monitoring not to be cast in the role of parent or be viewed as the "porn police." Continuing to monitor does not allow your partner to find his own internal observer—a skill that is vital to his personal recovery. Ultimately, if you do not feel you can trust your partner enough not to monitor him, you also do not have enough trust to build true intimacy.

Exercise: Write a Love Letter

As you begin to come through the storm of the crisis of the discovery of sexual compulsivity, it is now clear that your relationship has deeply altered. Although your connection to your partner may still feel a little shaky, if you're still reading, we can assume you have begun to deepen your intimate connection. This is a moment to reflect on what you appreciate about your partner. What are the qualities you admire? How does your partner support you in ways for which you are thankful? In what ways does your partner bring out the best in you? What do you love about your partner?

Sit down and take as much time as you need to write down the ways in which you feel gratitude for your beloved. This is a moment to remain focused simply on the gratitude, on your appreciation and your acknowledgement of that appreciation.

After you have both written your gratitude notes, your love letters, share them with each other. When you do this sharing, we recommend that you set aside an entire evening to spend time just with each other. This is an evening to simply relax, sit back, and reflect on how far you have traveled together.

CHAPTER SUMMARY

- Although there can be what seems like unbearable pain in the process of deepening intimacy, this crisis is transforming both you and your relationship.
- The deepening of love and intimacy requires the willingness to make the needs and wants of the other, and of the relationship, just as important as your individual needs and wants.
- The viewpoint of your partner can help you see more clearly into your individual style of self-protection—a protection that actually keeps you away from intimacy.
- Intimate conversation is built on two skills: reflecting and expressing compassionate understanding. Reflecting is simply putting what your partner has said to you in your own words. Compassionate understanding is expressing whatever awareness you can find about your partner's experience—not to change it, to fix it, or to correct it, but simply to acknowledge that it exists.
- Compulsive addictive sex can be thought of as simply remaining focused on the sex act itself. Intimate sex brings love, connection, compassion, and intimacy into the picture, that's why it is called making love.

Looking Forward

Chapter 11 will help you determine if you need outside support as you work with the issues of sexual compulsivity in your relationship. There are resources listed for finding help through groups, individual counseling, or further reading.

CHAPTER 11

Finding Support When You Need It

Whether individually or as a couple, you may need or want to seek outside support in the form of counseling, groups, or additional self-help books. You are not alone. Millions of others have sought support from groups and counseling. This chapter is primarily informational to better prepare and enable you to take what can feel like a big step of attending a support group or contacting a counselor. See Appendix A, "Additional Reading," for a list of reading materials.

Support Groups Related to Sex Addiction

As mentioned in Chapter 1, human beings need and want human connection. When you are grappling with an issue or problem or fumbling your way through a painful period in life, there are thousands of others who are or have been in a similar situation. What you might learn from their experiences can help ease any sense of isolation you may have. In addition, when you attend a support group, it is not just you who is benefitting from others; they are also benefitting from you and your experiences.

The following is a brief description of groups and associations related to sex addiction and co-sex addiction. We encourage you to go to the websites to learn more details about the groups, their members, and their meetings. If you do not live near a city, many of these groups have both telephone and online meetings in which you can participate anonymously.

SAA—Sex Addicts Anonymous—*www.saa-recovery.org*

Sex Addicts Anonymous is based on the Twelve Steps of Alcoholics Anonymous. It has meetings open to anyone who wants to find out more about recovering from addictive behaviors and closed meetings that are available only to those who have decided to stop their addictive sexual behavior. There are also conference-call telephone meetings and online web meetings. One way to find out more about Sex Addicts Anonymous is to read their online pamphlets at *www.saa-recovery.org/SAALiterature.*

SA—Sexaholics Anonymous—*www.sa.org*

Sexaholics Anonymous is a recovery program based on the Twelve Steps principles of Alcoholics Anonymous. Men and women "share their experience, strength, and hope with each other that they may solve their common problem and help others to recover. The only requirement for membership is a desire to become sexually sober. There are no dues or fees for SA membership."

COSA—Co-Sex Addict Anonymous—*www.cosa-recovery.org*

COSA is an anonymous "twelve-step recovery program for men and women whose lives have been affected by another person's compulsive sexual behavior." COSA is open to anyone who has been affected by sexually compulsive behavior. There are face-to-face meetings listed by state on the website. There are also telephone meetings in which COSA members participate anonymously.

SLAA—Sex and Love Addicts Anonymous—*www.slaafws.org*

SLAA is "a Twelve Step, Twelve Tradition oriented Fellowship of men and women who help each other to stay sober. We offer help to anyone who has a sex addiction or love addiction or both and wants to do something about it." Members strive to have a special understanding of each other and the disease as they go through recovery. SLAA has in-person meetings worldwide. There are also telephone and online meetings.

RCA—Recovering Couples Anonymous—
www.recovering-couples.org

RCA is an association of recovering couples "committed to restoring healthy communication and caring and, as we do this, we find greater joy and intimacy."

SCA—Sexual Compulsiveness Anonymous—
www.sca-recovery.org

SCA is a Twelve Step fellowship that is open to individuals of all sexual orientations with a desire to recover from sexually compulsive behaviors. SCA meetings are "not group therapy, but a spiritual program that provides a safe environment for working on problems of sexual addiction and sexual sobriety." To learn more about what happens at meetings as well as locations in the United States and around the world, go to the SCA website.

SRA—Sexual Recovery Anonymous—
www.sexualrecovery.org

Similar to other groups, SRA uses the Twelve Steps and is open to men and women seeking to share experiences as they work to solve the common issues regarding sexual addiction. The SRA website lists areas where there are meetings. You can also learn the process of starting an SRA meeting in your area. The website also has a pamphlet showing a typical meeting format.

S-Anon International Family Group—*www.sanon.org*

S-Anon is a program of recovery for those who have been impacted by the sexual behavior of another. It is based on the Twelve Steps and Twelve Traditions of Alcoholics Anonymous. S-Anon Family Groups are composed of "relatives and friends of sexually addicted people who share their experience, strength and hope in order to solve their common problems." There are no dues and the locations of meetings in countries around the world can be found on the S-Anon website. Before attending a meeting, it is advisable to look at the questions and answers regarding meetings at *www.sanon.org/meetings.htm.*

Consider Counseling

You may want to seek counseling as an individual desiring to change your sexually compulsive behavior, as the spouse or significant other of a sex addict, or as a couple wanting to understand or strengthen your relationship. Professional counselors work with individuals, couples, and families to identify problems and provide potential solutions. During in-person or telephone sessions, you can examine behaviors, thoughts, and feelings to determine sources and resolutions for problem areas in your life.

People often find excuses why they don't have time for counseling, or say that their partner won't cooperate, or believe that it's hopeless. In our experience, whether you go with your spouse or not, or whether your spouse cooperates or not, counseling can be of great benefit to you. If a couple does go together, the relationship has a greater chance for surviving and deepening into greater intimacy.

When to Seek Counseling

At what point do individuals and/or couples typically decide to pursue counseling? To find the answer, there are questions to ask yourself and signals to which you might pay attention. A brief list follows:

- You or your partner wants to stop sexually compulsive behavior but have not been successful
- Discussion about sexually compulsive behavior leads to unresolved arguments
- One or both partners feel betrayed by the other
- One or both partners feel distanced or shut out by the other
- Children are negatively impacted by behavior or negative feelings of the parents
- Frequent mention of divorce
- Poor communication in general, such as "he/she doesn't listen"
- Emotional infidelity
- Not spending time together
- Additional addictive behaviors such as substance or alcohol abuse
- A recent change in the relationship, such as the discovery of infidelity, loss of job, or death in the family
- Difficulty concentrating at work

What to Expect During Counseling

Professional counselors conduct counseling sessions in person or over the phone. Sessions generally last fifty minutes to one hour. The counselor may encourage you individually or as a couple to do certain homework, such as making a certain time each day to honestly discuss your feelings. (Chapter 8 provided guidelines for such honest communications.)

Many people unfamiliar with counseling see it as the medical equivalent of going to a doctor and, therefore, expect to be finished in a few short visits. With psychological counseling, the timeline and frequency can be much longer. From reading the preceding chapters of this book, you probably realize that there are a lot of aspects to behavior, some of which originated in childhood. You are most likely familiar with what happens at an archeological dig, where an archeologist might sift through layers of sediment to find tiny fragments that add up to a portrait of life in a village thousands of years ago. Similarly, it may take you and your counselor time to piece together the information from your life and the life of your significant other for a greater understanding of present-day behavior to occur.

By uncovering clues from your past, you and your counselor may identify what are called patterns of behavior. A pattern is a behavior you do over and over again, without being consciously aware of why you are doing it. Once you have identified patterns and where the behavior originated, you will not only have a better understanding of yourself (and your partner, if you learn about his or her patterns), you will also be able to consciously make different choices.

While this may sound very time consuming and even tedious, it can be an exciting adventure of discovery that can impact all areas of your life. The rewards can be great, such as feeling less conflicted and more relaxed, less isolated and more connected with others, with less anxiety and more enjoyment of life in general.

Where to Seek Counseling

You will find listings of counselors online and in phone books. The credentials of counselors may vary. There are psychiatrists who have been trained as medical doctors. There are psychologists who have been specifically trained in counseling or psychological therapy. There are many other counselors who also have specific training in certain areas, such as sexually compulsive behavior. We would encourage you not to judge a counselor solely by his or her university degrees or credentials. What matters most is that you feel comfortable and trusting with your counselor. You may already be aware that, just as with an attorney, what you say to your counselor is confidential.

The cost of counseling varies and the counselor should tell you the cost of each session beforehand. In some situations, but definitely not all cases, your health insurance will cover the cost of counseling. There are also community and city counseling programs where counseling sessions may be available at no cost or for a minimal charge.

You may be referred to a counselor familiar with sex addiction by a family physician, a member of the clergy, a friend, a crisis hotline, or, as mentioned above, online or in a phone book. When you do speak with a counselor, most likely initially on the phone, we encourage you to ask what type of counseling is being offered, if the counselor has experience with sexually compulsive behaviors, and what the costs are.

Many organizations list counselors online, and some of these specialize in sexually compulsive behavior. We recommend your first step be going to the website of the Society for the Advancement of Sexual Health, which has a directory of sex addiction counselors, medical institutions, and treatment facilities: *www.sash.net*.

Only You Know What's Best for You

Therapists and counselors generally practice psychology according to what they learned in college, and in accordance with the approach of a particular school of psychology. Many therapists then put their own interpretations, variations, and possible improvements into their style of counseling. The point is that, just as every person is different, every therapist is different. Just as you may feel comfortable with or trusting of some individuals and not others, you may find yourself sitting across from a therapist and feel put off or more guarded than usual. You may just have the feeling that something is not right. We want to encourage you to honor that feeling.

On the other hand, when you explore issues and problems, you are not necessarily meant to feel comfortable. Opening old wounds or recalling long-forgotten painful memories can be stressful. As the saying goes, "no pain, no gain." Although we do not believe that you need to re-experience pain, the process of counseling can, at times, be an unsettling and bumpy road. We are not advising you to stop counseling when you feel anxious and ill at ease; feeling uneasy can be a precursor to realization and change. What we are saying is that only you can discern when your discomfort is about your own growth and potential change, your relationship growth and change, or the approach, methodology, or attitude of your therapist. When you feel your discomfort is due to something about the approach of your therapist, it's time to consider finding another therapist.

When the Sexually Compulsive Behavior Is Illegal

If you or your spouse has been involved in sexually compulsive behaviors that could have legal consequences and you seek support from anyone in authority, that person will be required to report your behavior. Similarly, therapists are required by law to report actions that have caused harm to others. However, if you have committed such behaviors, you need help, preferably from a therapist trained in treating such behaviors. At the very least, you may seek support for recovery by anonymously participating in one of the above-mentioned groups, such as SA or SLAA. In addition, for issues of incest and child abuse, you or your spouse are strongly advised to contact Child Protective Services.

Many states have governmental agencies called Child Protective Services, or a similar name, such as Department of Children & Family Services or just Social Services. These agencies respond to reports of child abuse and can provide protection for a child as well as counseling for both the child and the child abuser.

Ellis and Serena: Seeking Support from a Group

Ellis and Serena had been married for only a year when Serena discovered that Ellis, a former athlete and now a scout for a major sports team, had been frequenting strip clubs while on the road. Ellis explained that, for business reasons, he needed to go to the clubs with prospective players. But Serena soon discovered that Ellis had not been telling the whole truth, which was that he was also going to these clubs by himself, paying for lap dances, and even sex. He told Serena he would stop the lap dances and sex.

However, he did not believe he had a problem, even though he went to strip clubs as often as possible, sometimes even during his lunch when he was not traveling. But Serena could no longer trust him. She had learned enough about sexually compulsive behavior to know that most men had difficulty stopping. She tried not to monitor his activities, and he tried to call her regularly when he was on the road. Yet, they were still at an impasse.

During one of Ellis's frequent trips, Serena found out the location and meeting times for a sex addiction group for couples. Ellis was resistant to attending. He said he would be away too often to be part of a weekly group. He protested that Serena should just try harder to trust him and, besides, he didn't really have time for a weekly meeting. That was when Serena angrily asked him if he had time for their marriage.

As they drove to that first meeting, Ellis and Serena were both nervous. Surprisingly, this created a sense of connection between them; they were sharing a new experience. Once at the meeting, Ellis and Serena both relaxed a little as they realized that their own relationship was similar to that of others. As Ellis heard the other men being open and honest about resisting their addictions to watching porn, frequenting strip clubs, or having anonymous affairs, he gradually began to feel that he could draw on his own self-discipline as he worked through the deeper reasons why he was drawn to sexually compulsive behavior.

Over time, through listening to the experiences of the women in the group and hearing the compassion and forgiveness they had for the men in their lives, Serena realized she had been very judgmental toward Ellis. She knew she could continue to keep him out in the cold for having cheated on her (and lying about it), or she could choose to strengthen their relationship. She began to shift from being an indignant spouse to a true partner in his recovery. This transition in Serena signaled a willingness to trust and share a deeper intimacy.

After they had attended these meetings for a few months, Ellis could sense the change in Serena. He told her that, although he enjoyed being a scout, he would ask if he could be transferred to the front office of the sports franchise where he worked. That way he could be home more.

Jason and Allison: Seeking Support from a Therapist

Married when they were both in their twenties, Jason and Allison were now in their mid-forties, and their two grown children were away at college. During the course of their relationship, Jason had battled alcohol abuse and eventually attended AA meetings. He had now been sober for eight years. Allison had also wanted him to stop smoking cigarettes, but Jason said that it was too difficult to stop. Gradually, over the years, between work, children, extended family, and social commitments, their relationship had lost its glow and become routine.

Although Allison was not aware of the change in their relationship, Jason had felt neglected, and he began to cope in the only way he knew how—through addictive behavior. Except this time it was sexually compulsive behavior. A friend at work had introduced Jason to his lunchtime activity of visiting a sexual massage parlor. Although he said he would try it only once, Jason was now returning to the massage parlor almost daily, and had developed feelings for one of the women who worked there. To her, Jason was only a customer, but part of her job was to play the role of a lover who cared about him. Jason was hooked.

When Allison was consistently unable to reach Jason on his lunch hour, she became suspicious. She confronted him and was hurt to learn of his behavior. Jason pleaded with her to understand, and swore an oath that he would never go back there. Instead, he soon found himself at another massage parlor, developing feelings for another woman. Although Allison took this as a sign that Jason's feelings for these women were not very deep, she was getting fed up with his behavior. In addition, there was the expense that this was adding to their monthly budget, an expense she realized Jason had kept secret from her by pulling money from their savings. She was furious with him.

When they discussed separation and divorce, Jason reacted with anger and sulking. He left the house in a huff and drove to a nearby tavern that he frequented in years past. He walked in, thinking, "The hell with her! I don't need her!" He sat down at the bar where a few of the old regulars recognized him. Seeing them, Jason realized that they had not changed, except for the toll that years of abuse had taken on their bodies. The bartender was also from the old days, and knew Jason was an alcoholic in recovery. He acted quickly, setting down a glass of ginger ale in front of Jason.

While still eyeing the bottles of alcohol on the shelves behind the bar, Jason sipped his ginger ale and listened to the old regulars. He heard about their operations and divorces. Now the bar was their family. Although there was nothing wrong with them having each other as drinking buddies and "bar family," Jason realized he had a family—a wife he did not want to lose. While driving home, he called Allison, told her what had happened, and agreed to go to counseling together.

They confided in their family doctor, who recommended a therapist who specialized in addictions, and especially in sex addiction. As they began their weekly counseling sessions, Allison and Jason both expressed their anger and frustration, which gradually gave way to compassion and forgiveness. Allison was able to understand how and why Jason had felt neglected, and Jason saw the origins of these feelings in his own childhood. Jason was able to stop his acting out, and Allison's love for him was renewed. They made time for each other. Although it took many counseling sessions, along with daily conversations, they were not only able to save their marriage but to strengthen it. After seven months of counseling, they decided to go on a second honeymoon to Hawaii.

Exercise: Are You Comfortable Seeking Support?

This exercise is to encourage you and your spouse to sit down together and have an open and honest conversation about your limitations. Is reading this book enough to shift the behaviors you and your spouse have been exhibiting? It may be. However, if the behaviors are too entrenched and it is too difficult to change, or if a third party is needed to meditate your conversations, it may be time to seek additional support, either through groups or counseling for couples.

Here are a few questions to ask yourselves:

- How long have we had this issue? (Remember to be completely honest.)
- What has the cost been in terms of our relationship, our time, our finances, our work, etc.?
- How long are we willing to continue to live with this behavior?
- Would hearing the experiences of others in groups be beneficial?
- Have we heard enough about others, either through reading books or watching TV shows, to know that what we really need is to see a counselor?
- If you have trouble deciding right now, it may help to review the previous chapters.

CHAPTER SUMMARY

- You may need or want to seek outside support in the form of counseling, groups, or additional self-help books.
- In attending a support group, what you might learn from the experiences of others who have been in a situation similar to yours can help ease any sense of isolation you may have. In addition, it is not just you benefitting from others; they are also benefitting from you and your experiences.
- You may want to seek counseling as an individual desiring to change your sexually compulsive behavior, as the spouse or significant other of a sex addict, or as a couple wanting to understand or strengthen your relationship.

Looking Forward

In Chapter 12, we will look at the spiral nature of navigating the journey of deepening your relationship and developing your capacities as an observer.

CHAPTER 12

The Journey Continues

As a child, you probably heard fairy tales that helped shape the foundation for your expectations of relationships. The movies and television programs you saw as a child created a particular fantasy image of domestic bliss. As you have grown, matured, and experienced life in relationships, the fantasy of that promise has been exposed. Especially since sexual compulsivity is a part of your relationship, you are traveling a particular path that is challenging, demanding, and painful, yet also contains the possibility for great growth and revelation.

Your capacities of courage, perseverance, faith, and strength have been tested. Please know that many, many people who have found themselves in a difficult relationship like yours have been able to navigate their way to a more loving partnership. We are not promising a happily ever after, but it is absolutely possible for you to deepen the love and support between you and your beloved. This does not mean you are going to reach some idyllic plateau where your relationship will have no difficulties. As it is with the weather, your life and relationship will continue to experience beautiful, sunny loving moments and those that are more stormy.

The Spiral

From the macro to the micro, life as we see and experience it is a spiral. From the shape of our galaxy to the form of our human DNA, our world appears in spirals. The experience of walking through a difficult time in a relationship can be unnerving because it brings up old feelings, wounds, or memories that you may have believed were resolved. Many individuals are surprised and dismayed that issues they thought had been thoroughly examined and resolved come flooding back. This can cause a feeling of going backward or of going in circles. Many have said, "I thought I'd already dealt with this" or, "I thought I had matured past the point of having to be in a situation like this."

In times like these, remember the spiral. You may be coming back around to face a type of issue you had previously experienced, but this time you are bringing the wisdom you gained from the earlier times you dealt with the same issue. Likewise, the skills, learning, and intelligence you are now gaining will be available to you the next time you traverse this part of your life's spiral.

The pain of living through this portion of your life can force a kind of focus and attention that you might not have otherwise experienced. What may seem to be the unbearable pain of moving through this time can bring great wisdom. What may look to be a hopeless situation in a relationship can bring the two individuals in the partnership closer than they previously knew was possible. We have watched couples come back from the brink of what they were certain was the end of their relationship.

We have heard it said that being in an intimate partnership is like attending relationship graduate school, participating in a master's class in partnering. We wholeheartedly agree! This kind of relating can require a level of awareness, attention, and surrender unlike any other life challenge.

The Observer

An understanding that often grows and deepens with difficulty in a relationship is the awareness of the observer. In Chapter 10, we discussed the need to develop your capacity for independence, your individual sense of internal strength, so that you have the resilience and durability needed to relate intimately. It is difficult not to feel overrun by your partner's feelings or emotions, by his or her wants and needs, when you are feeling fragile and defended. It is hard to be undefended enough to intimately merge with your partner when your defenses are telling you that you are in danger. When your protective mechanisms are telling you to be on red alert, it is difficult to surrender into intimacy.

A Fairy Tale

In an old German fairy tale, a beautiful young maiden is able to spin straw into gold with the magical aid of the gnome, Rumpelstiltskin. However, in payment for his magical assistance in spinning the straw into gold the beautiful young maiden has to promise to give the magical gnome her first-born child. Since this is a fairy tale after all, she marries the king and becomes queen of the land. When she and the king have their first child, the rascally Rumpelstiltskin appears to claim the baby. The queen offers all her wealth, but Rumpelstiltskin is set on taking the precious heir to the throne. The queen begs and begs, so Rumpelstiltskin finally makes a deal with the queen that if she can guess his name, he will not take the child. The gnome is certain that the queen can never guess such a complicated name as Rumpelstiltskin. Who could?

Since this is a fairy tale after all, the queen is true of heart, strong, courageous, and blessed. She is able to gain knowledge of the gnome's secret mountain hideaway and overhear him singing a song about his impossible-to-guess name. She thought that all was lost, but through her wisdom, strength, courage, and perseverance she was able to discover the secret needed to save what was most precious.

You have the capacity to spin the straw of this difficulty in your relationship into the gold of deeper connection. One way to accomplish this is to metaphorically step outside yourself and use your capacities as the observer. If you can watch yourself, you will have the opportunity to see that you do not have to react as you have in the past. You can make a different choice. Just like the queen in the fairy tale, your knowledge, strength, courage, and perseverance will show you what you need to learn.

One of the best ways to grow the capacity of internal strength is to develop your witness, your observer. You have the capability to observe yourself. Right now, check and see that you can be aware of your body, where it is in space. You can simply notice your body breathing. You can also observe any thought floating by in your mind about the words you are reading. You may or may not also be having some kind of feeling or emotion about the words. If you are, you can note this feeling or emotion. It is your observer that is aware.

Additionally, you have the capacity to notice the interplay of the sensations of your body, of your thoughts, and of your feelings and emotions. You can bring your awareness to how they interact. If you feel a pain in your body, your mind may be having a thought about it like, "That hurts, I don't like it." If your body is experiencing pain, you may also be having an emotional or feeling response to the pain. You may be having signals of fear about the physical discomfort, or you may be having an angry response.

You have the capacity to observe all of these connected inner workings. Focusing on the observer of these responses is like taking a step back to allow yourself to observe the pleasant or unpleasant scenery of this moment in your life.

In a moment, as you are observing your body, your thoughts, and your feelings and emotions, perhaps you can step back into your observer just a little further and ask yourself, "Who is observing this observer?" There is a quality of love, peace, and comfort available at the heart, the core of your observer. With the discovery of this secret, you will be able to loosen the tight grip of the intensity, even just for an instant, that your bodily sensations, thoughts, or feelings and emotions are serving up for your experience in this moment. Putting yourself in the role of observer has additional benefits, such as noticing when you have strayed from the path of kindness and compassion and have lapsed into shaming or blaming. Be as gentle and compassionate with yourself and with your partner as you can be. When you see that you have not been as gentle and compassionate as you wish you could have been, apologize as quickly as possible. It takes two to successfully navigate the difficult waters of a relationship. If you treat your partner with kindness and compassion, he or she is more likely to respond to you in a similar fashion.

Your Journey

This book is a compilation of the collective experiences of those who have walked along the path you are now walking. It contains wisdom gained from working through the trials of our own relationship as well as information gleaned from all the couples and individuals we have had the privilege of working with and knowing.

In Part 1 of the book, "Coming to Terms with Your New Reality," we have shared how to live through the initial discovery of the problem of sexual compulsivity in your relationship and basic facts about sex addiction. In Part 2, "Rebuilding Your Relationship," we explored skills and tools needed to put the pieces of your partnership back together and to deepen your relationship. Finally, in Part 3, "Moving Forward," we looked at ways to deepen intimacy and find outside support if you need it.

Although we present these skills as steppingstones, like a map, with each section building upon the previous one, in reality, your journey will occur in three dimensions. The elements of all of the skills interact and build upon each other. You and your partner will find your own path through the maze. You will create the map that is right for you and take the journey in your own unique way. Your willingness, compassion, and love for each other will help you find the answers embedded in your own questions. As the authors of these pages who have made a similar journey to greater awareness and deeper connection, we hope this book will serve as a guiding star to help you and your partner discover your unique path through the shadowy forest of relationship disorientation to arrive in the sunny clearing of true loving intimacy.

CHAPTER SUMMARY

- Since sexual compulsivity is a part of your relationship, you are traveling a particular path that is challenging, demanding, and painful, yet also contains the possibility for great growth and revelation.
- You may be coming back around to face a type of issue you had previously experienced, but this time you are bringing the wisdom you gained from the earlier times you dealt with the same issue.
- An understanding that often grows and deepens with difficulty in a relationship is the awareness of the observer.
- Many people who have found themselves in a difficult relationship like yours have been able to navigate their way to a more loving partnership. It is absolutely possible for you to deepen the love and support between you and your beloved.

APPENDIX A

Additional Reading

For more information about sexual addiction, relationship renewal, and related issues, consider picking up some of the following books.

Recommended Reading for Additional Support

Many excellent books provide valuable information on the origins, impact, and treatment of sexually compulsive behavior as well as related topics. The list below lists books you may find valuable.

Recovery from Sex Addiction

Breaking the Cycle: Free Yourself from Sex Addiction, Porn, and Shame by George Collins with Andrew Adleman.

In the Shadows of the Net by Patrick Carnes.

Out of the Shadows: Understanding Sexual Addiction by Patrick Carnes.

Thirty Days to Hope & Freedom from Sex Addiction by Milton S. Magness.

For the Partners of Addicts

Codependent No More: How to Stop Controlling Others and Start Caring for Yourself by Melody Beattie.

How Can I Forgive You? The Courage to Forgive, the Freedom Not To by Janis Abrahms Spring.

Relationships From Addiction to Authenticity: Understanding Co-Sex Addiction—A Spiritual Journey to Wholeness and Serenity by Claudine Pletcher and Sally Bartolameolli.

Sex, Lies, and Forgiveness: Couples Speaking Out on Healing from Sex Addiction by Jennifer P. Schneider and Burt Schneider.

On Relationship, Intimacy, and Sexuality

The Alchemy of Love and Lust: How Our Sex Hormones Influence Our Relationships by Theresa L. Crenshaw.

Attached: The New Science of Adult Attachment and How It Can Help You Find—and Keep—Love by Amir Levine and Rachel Heller.

The Couple's Guide to Intimacy: How Sexual Reintegration Therapy Can Help Your Relationship Heal by Bill and Ginger Bercaw.

Mapping the Terrain of the Heart: Passion, Tenderness, and the Capacity to Love by Stephen Goldbart and David Wallin.

Passionate Marriage: Keeping Love and Intimacy Alive in Committed Relationships by David Schnarch.

Undefended Love by Jett Psaris and Marlena Lyons.

Other Helpful Reading

The Drama of the Gifted Child: The Search for the True Self by Alice Miller.

The Gifts of Imperfection: Let Go of Who You Think You're Supposed to Be and Embrace Who You Are by Brené Brown.

How We Decide by Jonah Lehrer.

The Joy of Living: Unlocking the Secret & Science of Happiness by Yongey Migyur Rinpoche.

Women & Shame: Reaching Out, Speaking Truths and Building Connection by Brené Brown.

APPENDIX B

Bibliography

Abrahms Spring, Janis. *How Can I Forgive You? The Courage to Forgive, the Freedom Not To.* (New York, NY: HarperCollins Publishers, 2004).

Bader, Ellyn and Pearson, Peter. *In Quest of the Mythical Mate: A Developmental Approach to Diagnosis and Treatment in Couples Therapy.* (Florence, KY: Brunner/Mazel, 1998).

Beattie, Melody. *Codependent No More: How to Stop Controlling Others and Start Caring for Yourself*. (Center City, MN: Hazelden, 1992).

Bercaw, Bill and Ginger. *The Couple's Guide to Intimacy: How Sexual Reintegration Therapy Can Help Your Relationship Heal.* (Pasadena, CA: California Center for Healing, Inc., 2010).

Brown, Brené. *The Gifts of Imperfection: Let Go of Who You Think You're Supposed to Be and Embrace Who You Are.* (Center City, MN: Hazelden, 2010).

Brown, Brené. *Women & Shame: Reaching Out, Speaking Truths and Building Connection.* (Austin, TX: 3C Press, 2004).

Carnes, Patrick. *In the Shadows of the Net.* (Center City, MN: Hazelden, 2007).

Carnes, Patrick. *Out of the Shadows: Understanding Sexual Addiction.* (Center City, MN: Hazelden, 2001).

Collins, George with Adleman, Andrew. *Breaking the Cycle: Free Yourself from Sex Addiction, Porn, and Shame.* (Oakland, CA: New Harbinger Publications, 2011).

Crenshaw, Theresa L. *The Alchemy of Love and Lust: How Our Sex Hormones Influence Our Relationships.* (New York, NY: Simon & Schuster Inc.—Pocket Books, 1997).

Goldbart, Stephen and Wallin, David. *Mapping the Terrain of the Heart: Passion, Tenderness, and the Capacity to Love.* (Northvale, NJ: Jason Arnson, Inc., 2001).

Goldberg, Carey. "Marshmallow Temptations, Brain Scans Could Yield Vital Lessons in Self-Control." (*Boston Globe*, Boston, MA, October 22, 2008, Metro Section, A1).

Lehrer, Jonah. *How We Decide.* (Boston, MA, and New York, NY: Houghton Mifflin Harcourt, 2009).

Levine, Amir and Heller, Rachel. *Attached: The New Science of Adult Attachment and How It Can Help You Find—and Keep—Love.* (New York, NY: Penguin Group, 2010).

Magness, Milton S. *Thirty Days to Hope & Freedom from Sex Addiction.* (Carefree, AZ: Gentle Path Press, 2011).

Migyur Rinpoche, Yongey. *The Joy of Living: Unlocking the Secret & Science of Happiness.* (New York, NY: Three Rivers Press, 2007).

Miller, Alice. *The Drama of the Gifted Child: The Search for the True Self.* (New York, NY: Basic Books, 2007).

Pletcher, Claudine and Bartolameolli, Sally. *Relationships from Addiction to Authenticity: Understanding Co-Sex Addiction—A Spiritual Journey to Wholeness and Serenity*. (Deerfield Beach, FL: Health Communication, 2008).

Psaris, Jett and Lyons, Marlena. *Undefended Love*. (Oakland, CA: New Harbinger Publications, 2000).

Schnarch, David. *Passionate Marriage: Keeping Love and Intimacy Alive in Committed Relationships*. (New York, NY: Henry Holt and Co., Inc.—Owl Books, 1998).

Schneider, Jennifer P. and Burt. *Sex, Lies, and Forgiveness: Couples Speaking Out on Healing from Sex Addiction*. (Tucson, AZ: Recovery Resources Press, 2004).

Index

About the Authors

Paldrom Catharine Collins helps women and couples work through their sexually addicted relationships at Compulsion Solutions, an outpatient counseling service. Previously a Buddhist nun, she is married to a former sex addict. Her counseling focus has been to help individuals, couples, and groups find greater intimacy, more love, deeper peace, and more meaning in their closest relationships. She lives in Pleasant Hill, California. Find her online at *www.sherpacounseling.com.*

George Collins, MA is a former sex addict and the founder and director of Compulsion Solutions, an outpatient counseling service that addresses sexually compulsive behavior. George earned his master's degree in Counseling Psychology with a transpersonal specialization from John F. Kennedy University, and is a professional member of the Society for the Advancement of Sexual Health. He lives in Pleasant Hill, California. Find him online at *www.CompulsionSolutions.com.*